B 2 B

TECHNOLOGY MARKETING

HUGH TAYLOR

ISBN-13: 978-0615862941

ISBN-10: 0615862942

Taylor Market Intelligence, Inc. | www.hughtaylor.com

For all of my mentors.

CONTENTS

ACKNOWLEDGEMENTS

Writing a book is a large-scale undertaking. I wish to thank several people who have helped make this effort possible. My wife, Rachel, spent many hours proofing the manuscript, a labor for which I am deeply grateful. I am also indebted to my friend and colleague, Louise Elton, who copy edited the book. I have dedicated this book to my mentors, though, so I wanted to take a moment here to express my thanks to people who have helped me develop as a professional. My first mentor was the great film and television producer, Edgar J. Scherick, who taught me about storytelling and pitching ideas. As my career shifted into the enterprise technology field, I learned a great deal from Eric Pulier and Roberto Medrano of SOA Software. At Microsoft, I worked with many terrific people, from whom I learned a tremendous amount about planning and accountability. My Microsoft mentors include Yancey Smith, Jacob Jaffe, and Janice Kapner. At IBM, I had the privilege of working with some highly experienced technology product managers, including Heidi Ambler and Suzanne Livingston. In the startup arena, I owe a debt of gratitude to Jim McGovern, CEO of MediaPlatform, and Wendy White, VP of Marketing at Tier 3 and now my partner in Surge Marketing Group. Not everyone on this list was aware that they were mentoring me, but they were. Each of them pushed me to do my best work and continually improve myself. This book is my attempt to put all of the knowledge that I absorbed from working with these skilled and experienced individuals into a format that can be easily understood by others making their way in the B2B technology marketing profession.

FOREWORD

It is always an interesting feeling to finish writing a book and then realize, after you've put in the hundreds of hours of work, you still have more to say. I suppose this is the essence of writing. You are never completely finished. I am experiencing this now. As I conclude the writing and editing of *B2B Technology Marketing*, I find myself increasingly engaged with early stage technology ventures as a marketing consultant. I had been involved in this type of work on and off over the years, but as of 2013, this is becoming a big part of my working life.

Early stage technology ventures – those which are at the seed stage or "friends and family" level of funding – are a fascinating test bed for the concepts highlighted in this book. Most tech entrepreneurs are brilliant at engineering or starting tech companies, but they often need help in marketing. As I work through marketing strategy, positioning, messaging and go-to-market execution with these newly hatched companies, I find myself describing many of the ideas expressed in these pages.

If you're starting a new venture, or thinking about it, you might find this book to be a helpful guide to marketing. While I had originally intended this book to be for marketing professionals working at any size technology company – and the book is definitely relevant to marketers at all levels of the industry – the principles I write about here are particularly salient to startups. Startups have myriad challenges which can be addressed by this book. Startups need a marketing plan, regardless of their stage in life. Even when a product is being spec'd out on a whiteboard, someone needs to be thinking about marketing. Startups need help in marketing execution. Startups benefit from understanding how big tech companies approach marketing. Those big companies may become critical channel partners, so it helps to know what they want and how they work. Let this book be your guide to finding marketing success with your new venture.

Hugh Taylor

INTRODUCTION

Marketing technology products to business customers is a distinct discipline in the marketing profession, comparable to but quite different from consumer marketing and even mainstream business-to-business (B2B) marketing. B2B technology marketing presents many unique challenges to marketing executives, such as communicating the value proposition of a product that cannot easily be assigned to a particular product category. For instance, does a corporate video streaming tool belong in "Unified Communications" or "Collaboration"? It could be either, or both. Your job is to make people buy it. Yet, how can you sell a product that cannot be placed in a category understood by the buyer? The answer is "Yes, you can." This book gives you the foundation to be agile and adaptable enough to market enterprise technology products.

How I Came to be Writing this Book

The singularity of B2B technology marketing led to the creation of this book. I realized, after trying to explain what I did to countless product managers, engineers, investors, and partners, that my job was significantly different from what everyone else thought my job should be. This book was originally conceived as a series of long blog posts, a "blook" if you will. Over two years, I wrote one post a month and eventually compiled them into this book, give or take some editing after the fact. The project was rooted in my utter failure as a blogger. For some reason, though I can write with relative ease, the prospect of regularly creating posts of 500 or so words proved to be impossible; however, I **wanted** to blog. The social media marketing world of today demands it. So, what's a professional writer to do? Book writing is a more natural activity, given that I suffer from a disorder best expressed by Henry Kissinger, who said, "I can spend two or three hours on opening remarks." Short form communication just isn't for me.

A long time ago, at the very end of the *Mad Men* era, I worked in the printing business in New York City. (I'm not that old, but I knew a lot of agency guys in Manhattan in the late 1970s, who drank martinis at lunch, but I digress.) I made an observation at that time, which is that no one ever deliberately goes into the printing business. If you ask anyone who runs a printing business how they came to be in that occupation, you will invariably hear a story along the lines of, "Well... my brother-in- law got divorced. My wife had to take over this printing business, so now I'm running it." Or, "My father went to prison for tax evasion and I ended up with this printing business." No one ever says, "My dream in life was to own a printing plant."

Most of us fall into our careers. Or, they fall on us. I didn't set out to have a career in technology marketing, but a series of happy accidents has led me to where I am today. To be honest, some of those accidents didn't seem too happy at the time, but in retrospect they were meant to be. Over the last fifteen years, I have worked within marketing at a range of technology companies. I've been at several startups, including one which I partly owned, as well as at two of the world's largest technology companies. I've also been at one mid-sized enterprise software company. This has been a dizzying experience, but one which has given me a distinct grasp of what it takes to be successful in bringing a technology product to market.

My career yo-yo has taken me from being a generalist running the whole marketing department for a $2 million business, to being one of hundreds of people in the marketing group for Microsoft Office, the world's best-selling software. In the latter role, where I was managing public relations for SharePoint Technologies, I had a budget of over $1 million just for PR, a significant multiple of my entire marketing budget at the small startup. Making effective technology marketing happen in both settings was a very valuable experience for me. I learned that the core challenges of technology marketing are the same, regardless of size or scope of the organization. However, as a marketing organization grows larger and serves bigger corporate clients, the management challenges pile up quickly. My goal with this book is to convey an understanding of those core issues, but then illustrate how they can be managed given organizational complexities in larger teams.

Inside the Book

This book is divided into two segments. The first two thirds of the book (chapters 1-9) covers the basics of technology marketing and lay out the essential tasks and responsibilities of a B2B technology marketer. The final three chapters discuss the specifics of B2B technology marketing implementation. The book starts with a broad overview which asks and attempts to answer the question, "What is B2B Technology Marketing?" It then progresses through a review of the major responsibilities and challenges in the field and concludes with some practical highlights of how to put theory into practice. Here is what you can expect to learn:

Chapter 1, *Overview of B2B Technology Marketing*, contrasts B2B technology marketing with its cousin, consumer marketing. This introductory chapter establishes the role and mission of B2B technology marketers. The "Ten Commandments" of technology marketing outlined in Chapter 1 give an overview of the entire B2B tech marketing process.

In Chapter 2, *Create a Strategic Message for the Company*, we dive right into one of the thorniest issues B2B technology marketers face: Creating messages for your product and company that will have the desired market impact. Developing a strategic message is one of those processes, which is at once simple but potentially very tricky. All of the flaws and pitfalls in the B2B technology marketing discipline come out to attack you when you're trying to say exactly what it is that your company does, and why it should be the preferred choice for whichever category you serve. Chapter 2 offers some practices and templates to smooth the process.

Chapter 3, *Fill the Pipeline* and Chapter 4, *Create Preference*, pivot into pragmatic territory. Generating demand for your company's products and services is one of marketing's key missions. You have to supply the sales team with a steady stream of qualified prospects. Of course, what you might consider qualified may be quite different from what sales wants. Chapter 3 discusses how to define a qualified lead and resolve the potential dispute that may emerge with sales. Creating preference is a related activity. Defining sales as a process which begins with awareness and ends with being selected for purchase, Chapter 4 then goes into detail on how to convert someone who is merely considering your product into a real buyer. The two chapters work together as a unit, as the lead generation and preference creation processes are deeply linked. B2B tech marketers attract leads by raising awareness and using potential drivers of preference, such as unique features, to bring prospects into the sales process. To be selected, your product must be the preferred choice above all others. Thus, with the prospect in the pipeline, marketing needs to help sales make the case for preference and eventually, selection.

Chapters 5 and 6, *Understand the Industry and the Market*, and *Understand the Customer*, take a deeper dive into the process of mapping the mind of the customer and the dynamics of your industry. We revisit some of the category definition challenges discussed in the strategic messaging section. Chapter 5 also sets out some practical thinking on how to determine an accurate market size for your product. Useful, correctly scaled data on markets is rare in B2B tech marketing – another factor which makes the discipline distinct from other forms of marketing, where reliable industry data is a given. In tech, it is far from certain that anyone has correct information about the market. Why? Because, for the majority of tech products, markets are evolving so they are difficult to segment clearly. A related quandary: There is no "customer" in B2B tech. There are invariably committees of stakeholders who form in an erratic buying cycle. Thus, while understanding the industry and customer might seem like marketing 101, in B2B tech they are anything but that. They are among the most sophisticated challenges you will ever face.

The last three chapters of the book's first section cover situations where marketing interacts with other areas of the business. Chapter 7, *Inform Product Design*, is about product marketing. This the process by which the marketer solicits feedback from customers and other research subjects and gives input to the engineering and product management teams. Chapter 8, *Advise Senior Leadership on Corporate Strategy and Organization*, takes this concept to a higher level. Marketing people can and should have a voice in the overall direction of a technology business, whether the business is a startup or a unit of a larger concern. B2B marketing in technology is closely aligned with business strategy, as evolving markets typically define the strategic business opportunity. Chapter 9, *Marketing in a Sales Support Role*, discusses the practical but sometimes contentious topic of what marketing's obligations are to the sales team.

The second part of the book, Chapters 10-12, deals with implementing the marketing processes described in the earlier chapters. Chapters 10-12 discuss issues surrounding implementation and offer suggestions for approaching the task of implementing a marketing plan. Chapter 10, *Implementing the Strategy Part I – the Marketing Organization*, explores the different ways a marketing department can be structured. The shape of the department, or the matrix it functions in, has a lot to do with how you actually execute marketing. In large organizations, for example, the matrix of marketing and other departments, such as channel management and sales, can affect the very essence of the marketing strategy. Chapter 10 also covers topics such as staffing and outsourcing, as well as issues such as where to place Web marketing and social media within a marketing organization.

In Chapter 11, *Implementing the Strategy Part II – Planning and Budgeting*, we discuss a fundamental and critical aspect of managing marketing at a technology company. We describe a commitment and score carding process which can be an effective way of establishing goals and aligning everyone's efforts in marketing and related departments. We review ways to devise and validate plans and budgets amongst department stakeholders and internal clients. The intent is to help you understand the typical shape of the planning and budgeting process and how you can apply it to your particular situation.

Finally, with Chapter 12, *Implementing the Strategy Part III – Into Action*, we dig deep into the real work of implementation. Of course, this entire book is about doing the work; but here, when we talk about getting "into action," we mean how you will specifically organize the people on your team to execute the plan. Chapter 12 covers such topics as creating an ongoing task management deck, which connects with a marketing calendar with an eye toward ensuring that everyone on the team knows what has to be done at any given time. We talk about accountability and meetings, assigning ownership of projects, and tracking progress on a personal and team level.

At several points in the book, I comment that the topic we are discussing could be the subject of a whole book. Indeed, books have been written out of what I cover in a single chapter or even a couple of paragraphs. This book is not meant to be exhaustive in every category. I want to introduce you to many subjects, not overwhelm you. My hope is by reading this book, or the sections which are of interest, I will enable you to become a better B2B technology marketer. Developing real expertise in any given discipline requires real work on your part. My goal is to provide you with some information, insights, and tools that you can use to get yourself going in the field.

Chapter 1: Overview of B2B Technology Marketing

What is B2B technology marketing all about? It ought to be easy to explain what I spend my entire workday doing, but this is challenging. I find it particularly challenging when trying to describe my job to people outside the industry. You've heard of the "elevator pitch"? I have one of those. It goes like this: "I do technology marketing. I help my company find opportunities to sell its technology and support the sales teams with marketing materials and messaging." I even have what I call my "In-Laws Pitch," which is for people who need to know what I do in 10 words or less. That is, "I try to convince big companies to buy software." It's even difficult to explain technology marketing to some of my closest colleagues in sales and engineering. What do technology marketers do?

Part of the problem is that B2B technology marketing encompasses myriad combinations of responsibilities and organizational structures. Some of us are generalists who do it all. Others, such as product marketers or analyst relations people, are specialists. I've found that the best way to describe technology marketing is to work from a good example of what the discipline is supposed to be all about.

A Kilo of Gold?

Unfortunately, our professional discipline has a tendency to produce marketing pieces of some mediocrity. (I'm not exempting myself from this condemnation, either). Throw a rock, or a browser, and you will surely find an awful bit of technology marketing. I randomly selected a major technology magazine site and was greeted right away by the following banner ad from IBM, shown in Figure 1.

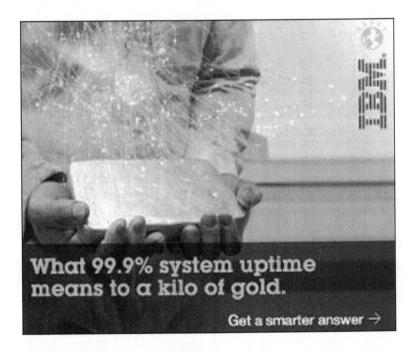

Figure 1 Example of an online ad for IBM

In the interest of full disclosure, I need to confess that I worked for IBM for a while. IBM in general has superb marketing and branding. However, once in a while as we see here, they get a little lost. What does 99.99% uptime mean to a kilo of gold? Personally, I don't know. Kilo of gold. Uptime. I'm missing the connection. The message is confusing except perhaps to someone who understands what the gold industry does with its infrastructure. Or, it might have something to do with green computing and its effects on gold processing. Who knows? Then the ad compounds its error by stating, "Get a smarter answer." Really? I would settle for *any* answer. And, if I thought I knew the answer, IBM is asserting, as they often do – that it's smarter than me. The IBM logo is capped by a golden globe, an icon of its "Smart Planet" campaign. The kilo of gold has something to do with getting the planet to be smart. This will be accomplished by patronizing IBM.

Let's be fair to IBM. They are trying to what all technology marketers do, which is to use an intriguing hook to get inside the headspace of a technology buyer; this is the essence of technology marketing. We are in the business of attracting buyers to our products using clever messaging and then invading this buyer's mind. We are influencers of thought processes. Our goal is to get inside the buyer's head and push the buyer down the path toward considering, preferring, and selecting our product over all others. The IBM ad, strange and off-base as it may be, is the first jab in this long process.

The Gold Ad, In-depth

The goal of the ad is presumably to intrigue the viewer and entice him or her to click on the link. The link will deliver the viewer to a page of IBM resources which explain the company's advantages in system uptime. And, as we know, there are few companies in the world superior to IBM in this department. The hook fails though, at least for me.

The actual call to action, "Get a smarter answer," is also a misfire for several reasons. Because the true answer is not clear, it doesn't make any sense to offer a "smarter answer." In order for there to be a smarter answer, there needs to be a less smart answer, which is clearly evident. Or, at least, there needs to be some conventional wisdom which the ad is challenging the viewer to rethink. Turning conventional wisdom on its head is one of the great pillars of technology marketing. This is also one of its most serious weaknesses, as most people are quite comfortable with conventional wisdom, even if it is inaccurate.

If the ad said something like, "Is 99.9% system uptime mission critical?" and then suggested you could find a smarter answer, which would at least hold up in logical terms. It would intrigue. You might think, "Hmm… is there something better than 99.9% uptime? Is there a better way of measuring system uptime?"

But, the ad is a bit insulting. It says, in effect, that your little brain can only come up with a dumb answer. You're so dumb, you need IBM to help you do your job. You'd be dumb to not work with IBM. This is not good messaging. Plus, why would anyone want a "stupid answer" to a big IT question? Of course people want a smart, or smarter answer.

Another problem with this ad is its unfortunate fusion of corporate and product-level messaging. If you've been reading the newspaper in recent years, you surely will have seen the IBM *Solutions for a Smarter Planet* campaign. This campaign is a corporate level, broadly-based series of messages, which suggests that IBM technology can essentially improve the world. IBM technology can make government systems, the environment, corporate life, and so on, smarter and better. Whether or not this is true, I don't know, and I don't think anyone will ever prove IBM right or wrong. However, its marketers developed a clever advertising campaign in that it speaks to the buyer-seller dialogue so common in IT marketing. The campaign is aimed at the CIO, CFO, and CEO. IBM is very strategic in this way. They go straight to the top and overrule so many competing vendors. Yet, this is part of the ad's problem. It is speaking to the wrong people.

Buyers who are interested in system uptime are generally not as focused on the welfare of the planet as the CEO might be. This is a "nice to have" aspect of a technology buy, to be helping the planet get smarter, but for most technology buyers, the immediate requirements are much more compelling. IBM usually segments its product advertising carefully by brand. Lotus is yellow. WebSphere is purple, etc. This ad probably belongs in the green logo'd infrastructure system group, but its gold. Here is another disconnect. It doesn't have the standard IBM brand signifiers, so this is visually confusing. The ad fails on almost every level.

The Role of Marketing in the Technology Business

Marketing in the technology field is a distinct discipline. It is similar to marketing in other spheres, but different enough to warrant extensive discussion. To frame the discussion, though, it makes sense to digress briefly into a general definition of marketing. From a solid, broad understanding of what marketing is, we can then look at marketing in technology with a more informed mindset.

What is marketing? It seems as if everyone knows what marketing is but cannot explain it very well. Marketing is so pervasive in our daily lives that simply defining it can be difficult. Marketing is on the radio, TV, billboards, Internet, and t-shirts. Marketing is on every piece of product packaging we see. We are exposed to thousands of marketing messages every day. Defining marketing is like defining air.

The omnipresence of marketing leads some people to trivialize it. "You're just the marketing guy," is a phrase I have heard uttered both outwardly and implicitly for many years. Marketing is not serious, some people would believe. It is the fluff, the pretty stuff that doesn't really matter the way, say, engineering or sales matters to a business. Yet, marketing is a serious function. Some aspects of marketing are fluffy or creative, but the core of marketing is critical to the growth and survival of a business.

So, again, what is marketing? Marketing is everything you do to place your product or service in the hands of potential customers. It involves understanding what your customer wants and then helping create the product or service which fits those desires. After that, the marketer has to price and package it, communicate with potential customers about it, and enable sales people and channel partners to sell it. How trivial is that? Not very…

The Four Ps

One way to get a handle on what marketing is all about is to think about the classic "4 Ps." As taught in most introductory marketing courses, there are 4 "Ps" to marketing a product or service:

- **Product** – What are you selling?

- **Price** – How much will the customer pay for it?

- **Place** – Where can the customer buy it? Meaning, is the product available directly, through a distributor, online, in a store, and so on?

- **Promotion** – How does the customer learn about it, and what incentives are created to buy it?

The Four Ps, Illustrated

The ad for the BMW 3 Series Convertible in Figure 2 gives us a great snapshot of the 4 Ps in action:

20

- **Product** - BMW 3 Series Convertible

- **Price** - $38,000

- **Place** - Your local BMW dealer

- **Promotion**
  - ○ Website
  - ○ Messages "Open for Inspiration" and "Joy is BMW"

Why the 4 Ps Matter

You might wonder why the 4 Ps are a big deal to marketers. Without getting hung up on the protocol, you need to think through all four elements in order to do any effective marketing. Think about it. You cannot market a product if you don't have a product (I'm talking to you, software industry!) You can't market a product if you can't say how much it will cost, have a place to sell it, or a way to promote it. If any one element is missing, the marketing effort is badly compromised or even impossible to execute.

When you plan a marketing campaign, you can use the 4 Ps as a guide. What will you be selling? What will it cost? How will you promote it? Where will it be sold? You have to be able to answer those questions before you can bring a product to market. Having an ambiguous or unsatisfactory answer to a "P question" means you have work to do before you go to market. If your "Place" involves selling both directly and through distributors, you will need to make sure you are not creating channel conflict by competing with your distributors. How will you work this problem out? There are many ways to fix channel conflict, but you need to understand that this is an issue before you can move ahead.

The 4 Ps also provide a great context for thinking about several other critical elements of the marketing process, namely the "Cs," which include customer, competition, and communication. There are dozens of "Cs" in the marketing business, ranging from "community" to "commitment." I am going to leave those on the side for now and focus on the big ones:

- Who is your customer?

- Against whom are you competing?

- How will you connect with the customer? By communicating a message which differentiates you from the competition.

Figure 2 - BMW Web Ad showing key branding messages.

What Marketing Messages Can Tell Us about the Customer

There are two messages in the BMW ad, shown in Figure 2. One says, "Joy is BMW" while the other states, "Open for Inspiration." These messages have a lot in common, though they differ in a critical way. "Joy is BMW" is a corporate branding message. It is about the BMW as a global automotive brand. It's about how BMW helps drivers enjoy their cars and the whole driving experience. This is similar to earlier versions of the message such as, "The Ultimate Driving Machine." The second message, "Open for Inspiration," is a product-level message. It's about the convertible, which is an "open" car.

What the two messages have in common is a visionary and aspirational quality. They are indirect and appeal to emotions about cars and driving. A generic approach to marketing a car would say something like, "A great car that gets you places and doesn't cost too much." Joy and inspiration are life experiences which many people seek on their paths to personal fulfillment. What they have to do with cars is a good question. I personally don't get such a thrill from my car (a Toyota) but perhaps my problem is that I don't drive a BMW. Maybe if I drove a BMW I would feel more joy and inspiration in my life, or at least in my car.

I'm not making fun of BMW. They try to take the audience to a higher plane of thinking about cars. A BMW is an expensive car, and the company realizes that an emotional connection with the buyer will help move the purchase decision along to an actual buy. Why does one buy an expensive car? If you just needed to get from point A to point B, you could spend about $15,000 on a set of wheels and be totally satisfied. Why would someone willingly spend more than twice this amount for what is essentially the same end product? Are those leather seats, fancy curves, and better engine really worth an extra $23,000?

The answer, of course, is yes. Those extras - the whole experience of owning and driving a BMW - is worth the money to those who buy BMWs. People who value such features and experiences are potential customers of BMW. The company has crafted its messages to reach this distinct customer group. People who can afford to get joy and inspiration from driving are not shopping for economy models. They want something more.

Messaging reveals how the marketer is thinking about its customers and competitors – the Cs mentioned earlier. When you combine the four Ps with the Cs, you have a more complete picture of what marketing is all about. **Marketing is a process of bring a product, at a certain price, to a certain place, with a promotion – all of which are geared to attract a certain type of customer and create preference over competing products.** Each element must be aligned in order for marketing to be successful. Table 1 summarizes how the elements work together. If you're doing your job as a marketer, you will see a natural alignment between the elements.

Table 1 – The 4 Ps for the BMW ad.

Product	Price	Place	Promotion	Customer	Competitor
BMW 3 Series Convertible	$38,000	Dealership	Website "Joy is BMW" "Open for Inspiration"	Luxury car buyer	Mercedes Jaguar Lexus

In Table 2, let's try to imagine what a marketing campaign would look like if the Pc and Cs were out of alignment.

Table 2 - The 4 Ps, deliberately out of alignment, for a hypothetical Toyota Corolla ad.

Product	Price	Place	Promotion	Customer	Competitor
Toyota Corolla	$80,000	Online orders only	"Corolla. The ultimate you. Accept no substitute."	Luxury car buyer	Ford Honda Hyundai

I have deliberately misaligned these elements to make my point. A Corolla is not an $80,000 car. How interested would a luxury car buyer be in an

$80,000 Corolla? And, even if the buyer were interested, what if the car were only available as an online purchase, with no test drives allowed? There is a certainty you would sell no Corollas online for $80,000 each. If you would, please contact me right away so we can start an online car dealership.

The promotion, too, is out of whack with reality. The Toyota Corolla, despite being a fine car, is not the type of automotive product which one would associate with "The ultimate you." The Corolla's actual slogan is, "Performance, Style, Safety... Pick Three," which is a clever fusion of facts and vision. Like the BMW message, the Corolla message brilliantly targets a specific type of car buyer. The marketing people at Toyota have researched who their buyers are and understand that the Corolla buyer is someone who wants good value from a car, but is willing to pay a bit more for safety and style.

Table 3 – Breaking out the 4 Ps and related marketing approaches.

	Product	Price	Place	Promotion	Customer	Competitor
Pc and Cs	Toyota Corolla	$18,000	Dealerships	Performance, Style, Safety, Pick Three.	Economy car buyer who values style and safety	Ford Honda Hyundai
Marketing approach		Priced a bit above rock bottom	Widely available	Messaging intended to appeal to the value conscious, safety and style-oriented buyer	The car, as well as the marketing, are designed to fit this narrow segment	Corolla is positioned as being better on performance, style, and safety than the competitors. If a competitor wins on one factor, the other two can push the deal back in favor of Corolla.

Table 3 shows how Toyota's marketing people are probably approaching each of their marketing elements. For each P and C, there is a thought process and marketing strategy. The underlying concept here is that the marketing professional needs to understand who the customer is, what that customer values, and what will drive this customer to choose a given product over competing offers. With that knowledge in mind, the marketer can then fashion messaging, pricing, and product strategies. We will return to these topics again throughout this book.

The chart also introduces the notion of "positioning," which really should be the 5th P, but I don't want to disrupt decades of marketing textbook production by suggesting a 5th P. Positioning, however, is a powerful force in marketing. Positioning has to do with the overall impact of the Ps and Cs, forming the sum of all the Ps and Cs as a whole to fend off competition. In our example, Corolla is positioned as a great economy car, but with just a bit more style and safety and a slightly higher sticker price than the rock bottom competitors. The positioning anticipates the buyer's thought process. The buyer might think, "I want a cheap car, but I deserve better than rock bottom…I want just a bit more. Okay, Corolla looks like a good bet."

Marketing vs. Sales, Advertising, and Public Relations

When I tell people I "do" marketing, they often comment, "That's like sales, right?" Or, "So, you do advertising?" Well, yes and no. Marketing is related to sales, advertising, and public relations but it is not the same thing. To help explain the difference, I turn to S.H. Simmons, author and humorist, who made the following observation about marketing. "If a young man tells his date she is intelligent, looks lovely, and is a great conversationalist, he's saying the right things to the right person and that's **marketing**. If the young man tells his date how handsome, smart and successful *he* is - that's **advertising**. If someone *else* tells the young woman how handsome, smart and successful her date is —that is **public relations**." Marketing is customer-facing. It's about connecting with the customer and conveying a message that captures the customer's interest. Advertising is direct. It's about the advertiser. Public relations is indirect. It involves a third party expressing an opinion about the advertiser.

Marketing supports the sales process, encompassing advertising and public relations. However, advertising is not marketing, nor is public relations. Ideally, the disciplines are well aligned. Advertising should match marketing's messaging and assert its core value propositions – all in the name of making sales. Public Relations should land stories and create media dialogues, which advance marketing goals, also supporting the sales representative in the field.

Marketing is about saying the right things to the right person. Sales is about getting the right person to take the final and decisive action required. You can't have one without the other. Marketing without sales is just one big tease which goes nowhere, and benefits no one. Sales without marketing is a losing proposition. Yes, there are people who can sell anything to anyone, but most sales people need marketing to help them on numerous fronts. Sales people typically need marketing to identify the right people to sell to, provide the value proposition for the product, and in some cases, provider the product itself.

The mutual dependence can lead to a love-hate relationship between sales and marketing. We'll cover this topic on and off throughout the book but it is worth introducing here. In the typically dysfunctional sales-marketing relationship, the sales team decries marketing's inability to generate good leads and its incompetence at messaging. In the other direction, marketers tend to consider sales people to be lazy ingrates who can't close perfectly good leads or make any sense of a brilliant message. The truth is usually somewhere in the middle. Marketing can always do better with leads and messaging, while sales has to focus on closing the opportunities, which marketing has created.

The Ten Commandments of Technology Marketing

What is B2B technology marketing all about? What do we do all day? When we talk about the four Ps and the Cs, it is descriptive of marketing, but we are still being too vague about what we actually do to market technology products. We need to pivot and present the four Ps, and the other aspects of marketing in general, as specific work tasks. These will be explored in depth as we move forward.

Here are ten areas of work which are central to technology marketing. I'll call them the Ten Commandments of Technology Marketing. In no particular order, as each activity is critical in its own way and supports the others:

1. **Fill the pipeline** – B2B technology marketing's most basic purpose is to attract qualified leads for the sales people to convert into revenue. There are many ways to fill the pipeline, from lead generation events to search engine optimization (SEO) and Google pay-per-click (PPC) marketing. In addition, virtually every other activity described on this list of commandments supports filling the pipeline. If you're messaging properly, creating preference, building the brand, etc., you will generate interest in the product and attract sales leads.

2. **Create preference** – Creating preference is part of the bigger mandate for B2B tech marketers to lead the buyer though a cycle which starts with awareness and continues through preference, and finally, selection. However, preference is probably the most critical part of the process. Getting the customer's attention is an essential first step, of course. You won't have the opportunity to talk to them if they don't know you exist. The real test of a B2B technology marketer is whether he or she can engage enough with the customer to create a preference for the solution in question. Once preference has been established, moving to the final sale is

mostly up to the account team, though a lot of the hard work has already been done by marketing.

3. **Understand the industry and market** – All of the activities in technology marketing flow from an underlying sense of how the industry works, where it is headed, and how products perform in the market. A B2B technology marketer needs to become an expert and perpetual student of the industry and market segment that he or she serves.

4. **Inform corporate strategy through market awareness** – Marketing at a technology business is a more strategic function than in many other industries. The pace of market change and the rate at which new, popular products can take off all influence corporate strategy. The technology marketer should be an influencer of corporate strategy.

5. **Support sales** – Like it or not, your duty is to support the sales process. Sales cannot function without marketing support, even if they beg to differ. The technology marketer has to provide sales with product collateral and "air cover" in the form of news reports, press releases, analyst coverage, and written content. At a higher level, the sales team is bringing the sum total of the marketing effort to the customer as they seek business. The better your messaging, strategy, product input, and execution, the more easily the sales team can get in the door, make the pitch, and then close deals.

6. **Message the company** – What does the company have to say for itself? Company level messaging is a big responsibility of technology marketing. When Xerox says it is "The document company," or Kodak says "Take pictures. Further," they are describing the higher level mission of the company. They are not selling any particular product.

7. **Message the product** – Each product that you market will likely have a different message. At the very least it will have a variation on a common message. As a technology marketer, you will need to communicate the product message, connect with the customer's set of needs, and make a case for preference.

8. **Build the brand** – The corporate brand is also your responsibility. Brand is the sum of many other activities and messages. You are its custodian, for better or worse. Your marketing should resonate with the brand and add to its value. At the same time, poor execution in marketing can damage the brand.

9. **Inform product design** – Whether it is your explicit responsibility or not, as a technology marketer you need to have input on the design of your company's products. This is imperative for many reasons. For one thing, you will be responsible for bringing the product to market, so you need to make sure you feel confident that it will sell. As the marketer, you will have an informed understanding of the customer. You should communicate what you know about the customer to the product developers.

10. **Understand the customer(s)** – Ultimately, technology marketing is all about satisfying the customer. You must absolutely understand what is on your customer's mind, the stresses he or she is facing, and how your product can help reduce this stress. This is true of all marketing, but in technology marketing it is especially tricky, as you are typically facing a group of customer stakeholders, each with different needs and diverging ideas about what it will take to solve everyone's problems.

10 Ways that B2B Technology Marketing is Different from Consumer Marketing

There is a vast gulf separating the two disciplines, though nailing down the precise differences is challenging. Yes, the two disciplines are broadly similar. Marketing Coca-Cola is sort of like marketing Oracle Databases. Both activities are intended to make people buy a particular product. Both companies advertise, though in quite different ways. Both companies have brands and messages, and many other comparable organs of marketing, but the basic process and end results are highly divergent.

You might ask, "Why does this matter?" It matters because many marketing professionals mistakenly think that what works for consumer brands will work for technology. This is not always the case. A lot of expensive branding consultants will work with you on building your technology brand. They will tell you that brand is what counts in marketing, based on the truth that branding is the ultimate goal of consumer marketing. No offense to this group of advisors, but brand building is a relatively low priority for business technology marketing, especially for early stage companies.

One reason things can become so confused is because popular consumer technologies are regularly adopted in the enterprise - think iPhone, Twitter,

Facebook, etc. These products are consumer marketing successes and they rely on proven consumer marketing techniques, such as brand building. However, trying to learn from these successes and apply consumer branding to a business technology product is ill-advised. Of course, Apple has a world class brand, which helps them sell to business customers. Does this mean you should drop everything and try to build an Apple-like brand for your business technology product? It is probably not the best use of your time and resources, particularly for small or new technologies.

To help us think through how marketing technology to business is different from consumer marketing, here are 10 ways that the two disciplines differ:

1. **B2B vs B2C** – The most basic difference between consumer marketing and technology marketing to businesses - this is a B2B sale. You are selling a business product to a business customer. It is a categorically different experience and process. This may sound obvious, but this fact escapes a lot of folks who aimlessly (mis)apply consumer marketing techniques to B2B technology marketing.

2. **B2B is not lifestyle-oriented** – Much of consumer marketing has to do with creating an affinity between a consumer, his or her lifestyle, and the consumer brand. This is a fantastic way to market cars, clothes, sporting goods, etc. However, it is not an effective way to market technology. There is a business technology version of "lifestyle," which we'll discuss in the next bullet, but it is different from the consumer approach to lifestyle branding.

3. **Tech buyers often have "religion"** – The technology version of "lifestyle" is what I called "religion." In the same way some people are die-hard snowboarders who swear by certain popular snowboarding brands, there are business technology buyers who have committed their careers and work days to a specific type of technology. There are Microsoft shops where people tend to favor Microsoft products over all others. IBM shops stay with Big Blue, and so forth. Alternatively, and this is where the "religion" may become intense, you have buyers who favor open source solutions over proprietary offerings. Technology companies market to these audiences in ways which tap into these affinities.

4. **Multi-buyer group** – In contrast to consumer marketing, which is almost always aimed at an individual, B2B technology marketing programs face a multi-buyer group in most situations. When you market technology products to business, especially big businesses, you need to convince a committee of buyers to select you.

5. **Long-term branding and short term incentives vs. a consultative, trust-based relationship** – Most consumer marketing is aimed at either long-term brand building or a short-term call to action, or some mix of the two. For instance, you might receive a coupon to buy a six pack of Coke if you act within a given period of time. This is a short-term incentive though it also helps build the Coke brand by repeating their name and slogan, for the billionth time, and making you think of them. Technology marketing is different. Yes, it has some of those basic elements, like repetition and presentation of a brand

message. However, technology marketing only works if the vendor can create a trust-based relationship with the client, one which is typically consultative in nature. Coke doesn't call you up and say, "What brand of soda is the right one for your life? Let's sit down and walk through a few soda-drinking scenarios and determine an optimal soda for you and your colleagues." It would be absurd, of course, but this is exactly how technology marketing succeeds. As the client develops trust in the vendor through a consultative process, the level of preference for their offering grows.

6. **Use of mass media** – Consumer marketing makes great use of mass media such as radio, TV, and outdoor advertising. Business-facing technology marketers should approach these media with great circumspection. TV and radio work well for products which rely on repetitive exposure to brand messages. Most technology marketers know better than to use these costly media for their offerings. You may see TV ads for major corporate technology brands, but these are mostly aimed at influencing wealthy people who own the stocks of these companies. (You'll see these on Sunday morning news shows.) Outdoor advertising is where some technology marketers fail with consumer-style mass media. In major cities, especially in the Bay Area, you can see billboards and bus shelter ads for all types of business technologies. There may be some value in these B2B tech ads in out-of-home signage but I question the marketing investment.

7. **Need for a business case** – Marketing technology to a business buyer invariably contains a business case for the solution.

Whether it is explicit and quantitative, or intangible, the technology marketing pitch involves explaining how the solution will improve the buyer's business. Typically, the solution is marketed as a cost saver, revenue generator, or enabler of smarter work – or a combination of all three. With the exception of energy saving features, consumer advertising seldom makes these types of claims. Consumer marketing is more emotional. Remember, "I'm lovin' it" for McDonalds? The jingle captures the emotional appeal of eating fast food at McDonalds. This approach doesn't work well in technology, though some have tried it. The IBM infrastructure campaign did use some humor as a hook to draw people into the idea of the "infrastructure nightmare" but the underlying pitch was very factual and business-oriented.

8. **Solution selling** – Business technology offerings are frequently composed of multiple solution components from different vendors, marketed as a whole. In contrast, consumer marketing is far more single-product or single-brand oriented. When you look at an ad for a Dell server, as a simple example, you are probably seeing marketing from Dell, Microsoft, and Intel all at the same time. Though you might see combined offers in consumer marketing, such as for Pepsi and KFC, we are not speaking of the same thing. Those server components *need* each other to make the sale. Not so with the chicken and soda.

9. **Value-added channels** – Technology marketing often involves channel partners, which add value to the solution. System integrators (SIs) and Value-Added Resellers (VARS) make their living by reselling and packaging multiple technology

components into solutions. Technology marketing has a great deal to do with how the channel is managed and motivated. Most consumer products also sell through distribution channels. You don't buy Coke directly from Coca-Cola, or even from the bottling company. However, the consumer channel does not typically add value the way the B2B technology marketing channel does. Would you expect a grocer to "consult" with you on what brand of soda to buy? However, you would demand an SI to advise you on the best kind of storage array to purchase.

10. **Lack of emotional loyalty** – Consumer branding is great at building emotional loyalty for the long term. A lot of us buy the same consumer brands over and over again because we feel an emotional connection to them. We like Coke, Budweiser, Jeep, and Marlboro. We've been encouraged - some would say "conditioned" - to prefer these brands through imagery and lifestyle associations. This preference is the result of intense investments in media. Technology marketing does not work this way. Yes, technology buyers often have strong preferences and brand loyalties, but they are generally not emotionally based. Technology buyer preference is usually driven by technical considerations, proven positive experiences, compatibility, or professional training. In some cases, the preference is based on a political perspective, such as with open source solutions. Technology marketers often make the mistake of thinking they can build emotional brand loyalty through repetitive advertising. This is possible, but difficult to do, and not a wise investment of marketing resources.

Chapter 2: Create a Strategic Message for the Company

Having reviewed B2B technology marketing in general, it is now time to tackle the work of creating a strategic message. The job may officially be the responsibility of an outside marketing agency. However, you are not off the hook on this important task. In my experience, you will have to provide guidance to that agency. You will have to understand the process of crafting a strategic message even if it's not your direct job.

Here is the challenge: The B2B buying process touches many facets of your company. The product, solution, and price combine with your overall reputation, and that of your people, to form a gut level impression and drive a "Buy/Don't Buy" decision. The customer's mindset in the decision transcends any rational analysis of each specific element. Fronting for this complete impression-making process is what I call a **strategic message**. Your strategic message articulates your company's essence and foundation of its value in the marketplace. It answers these and other questions:

- What business are you in?

- What do you do?

- What markets do you serve?

- Why are you (or could you be) a leader in those markets?

- Why are you valuable to investors or acquirers?

- How

- why are you a strategic success in the industry?

These questions stand by themselves but also overlap, as shown in Figure 3.

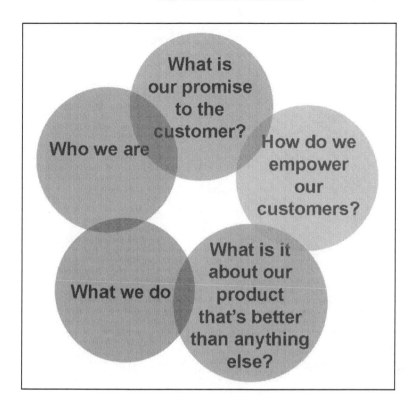

Figure 3 - Overlap of key questions posed by the strategic messaging process.

One thing to address right away is the differences between a strategic message and a message used in marketing a specific product or service – what's known as a "go-to-market" (GTM) message. While these message types overlap, they focus on different aspects of your business and have quite distinct purposes. Strategic messages are high-level and visionary, while GTMs are pragmatic and emphasize solutions and value propositions. Strategic messages advance the overall brand. GTMs advance the cause of the business unit/product/solution and business objectives (i.e. revenue/share). Strategic messages speak to industry level thinking. In contrast, GTMs focus on customer-centric thinking. Strategic messages are inclusive of all productions and solutions at a high level, but GTMs tend to stay on a single product set or solution. Strategic messages are often forward-looking, versus GTMs which are usually directed at immediate action. Strategic messages drive awareness of the company as a player in the industry rather than advocate preference for a specific type of purchase.

Exxon presents a great example of a contrasting strategic message and a GTM:

- Strategic message, i.e. "Who we are." - "We are the world's largest publicly-traded international oil and gas company, providing energy, which helps underpin growing economies and improve living standards around the world."

- GTM – "As the world's leading synthetic motor oil, Mobil 1 helps provide total engine protection and excellent fuel economy."

Consider the difference between the two. You don't pull into a gas station and ask for "energy to underpin growing economies." You ask for an oil change. You chose Exxon possibly because you heard that they have "the world's leading synthetic motor oil." Table 4 below goes into more detail on the differences between strategic and go-to-market messages.

Table 4 – Comparison of strategic and "go-to-market" messages.

Strategic Message	Go-to-Market Message
High-level, visionary	Pragmatic, solution-oriented value proposition
Advances the brand	Advances the business unit/product/solution business objectives (i.e. revenue/share)
Industry level thinking	Customer-centric thinking
Inclusive of all productions and solutions	Product and solution focused
Forward looking	Focused on today
Drives awareness of the company as a player in the industry	Drives preference for purchase of products and solutions
e.g., Exxon We are the world's largest publicly traded international oil and gas company, providing energy that helps underpin growing economies and improves living standards around the world.	e.g., As the world's leading synthetic motor oil, Mobil 1 helps provide total engine protection and excellent fuel economy.

To work, the message needs to be:

- **Comprehensible** – Will the target audiences understand the message?

- **Believable** – Will the claims made in the message be believed, or will the company look ridiculous for posturing in an unbelievable way?

- **Meaningful** – Does the message mean something specific to the target audiences? (i.e. If an analyst is reviewing competitors in a sector, will the strategic message create the desired impression?)

- **Aligned with go-to-market message** – Does the strategic message further the goals of the go-to-market message?

Technology Company Strategic Message Template

In the "trying to make your life easier department," I've devised a simple template for creating a strategic message. It goes like this:

The company innovates/leads/transforms the [market space] by producing [solution types] and leveraging [trends].

So, if I were asked to use this for Apple Computer (as they clearly need my help, you know…) I might come up with:

Apple Computer leads and transforms the personal digital device market by producing portable information technologies, which leverage consumers' increasing desire for ease of use.

Okay, maybe this is a bad example. If I had to do it for Microsoft's Server and Tools division, I would say:

Microsoft S&T is the corporate IT industry leader with extensive technology offerings, which leverage the trends of platform consolidation and reliable cloud computing.

Ready to try it for yourself now? Consider the forces that can shape the success of your message.

Forces which Affect the Success of a Strategic Message

Landing a successful strategic message with key audiences involves a delicate balancing act. There are many forces which can destabilize the impact of the message, and actually render it harmful to the Company's mission, and its objectives for the message. A strategic message is like a spinning top. A lot of things can pull it down. As Figure 4 shows, a successful message is like a top spinning **perfectly**. It receives positive reactions from key audiences without being pulled off its axis by messaging problems.

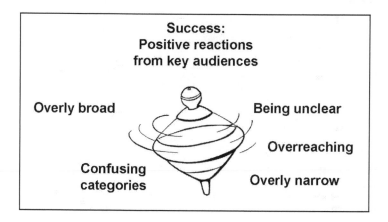

Figure 4 - Forces which can inhibit the effectiveness of a strategic message.

Factors which can pull a strategic message out its sweet spot include:

- **Being overly broad** – This is a classic strategic message pitfall, where you want to go for broad appeal but, in doing so, sacrifice tangible value. If you describe yourself as "an e-platform" or "a mobile lifestyle technology", you may not be not connecting the product enough with reality to make much of an impact on people.

- **Being overly narrow** – To avoid being excessively broad or up in the clouds, you might go too far in the opposite direction. Narrow messaging starts to look like a product-based GTM. If your strategic message says something like, "Better thermal characteristics for semiconductors," you're probably narrowing it down too much.

- **Category confusion** – Your message will land most effectively if you can situate your product accurately into a technology category. Being unclear about your category will blunt the impact of your message. Even worse would be creating a brand new category of your own.

- **Being unclear** – Vagueness is the curse of strategic messaging. Let's say your company makes software testing tools but you want a strategic message which connotes a broader value proposition. You come up with, "Powering reliability in the cloud." The problem with this message is that it could be describing hardware, operating system software, application software, testing software, or network infrastructure. You don't want to be vague about **what you actually do.**

- **Overreaching** – We all do this from time to time, but you have to watch out for overreaching in strategic messages. Sometimes your enemy here is the gerund, as in "Transforming mobile technology." Really? You're going to transform a hugely broad, multi-billion dollar category? This is excessive, even if it is a cool ambition to have. You don't want people to wonder what you're smoking when you considered your potential. The funny thing, of course, is that some companies truly attain goals which originally seemed impossible. If Facebook had based its early strategic messaging on the idea of revolutionizing social interactions amongst a billion users, it would have been laughable, but it would have been true.

Strategic Messaging Gotchas and Risks

Strategic messaging isn't easy. If it were, a lot more companies would have good strategic messages. This is not the case. There are several major "gotchas" at work when you try to devise a strategic message that truly lands where you have targeted. For one thing, the more credible and comprehensible you become, the more potentially narrow and small you look. Then, there is problem of market evolution. I like to say, facetiously, "If you can explain exactly what you do, then you're too late." All kidding aside, if a technology category is well-defined and understood, you have to work a lot harder to establish that you offer a unique value.

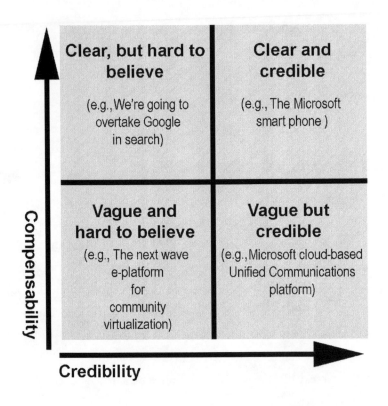

Clear, but hard to believe	Clear and credible
(e.g., We're going to overtake Google in search)	(e.g., The Microsoft smart phone)
Vague and hard to believe	Vague but credible
(e.g., The next wave e-platform for community virtualization)	(e.g., Microsoft cloud-based Unified Communications platform)

Compensability (vertical axis) · **Credibility** (horizontal axis)

Figure 5 - Balancing comprehensibility and credibility in strategic messaging.

Trying to be "hot" is a big pitfall. Technology which is old and boring is not hot. It is ice cold, and a big driver of low valuations and diminished interest in your company. Mainframe tools, anyone? So, you want to be hot. Who wouldn't want that? If you want to establish yourself as being in a hot category, you may need to define a category which either doesn't exist or is poorly understood. Or, to establish yourself in a new, hot category you may need to make claims that you can't back up, leading to possible credibility issues if the trade press wants to look into it. Consider, for instance, how to claim leadership in a category which either doesn't exist or isn't acknowledged by any respected third party? You will look as if you are full of malarkey. Latching onto hot trends without any meaningful unique differentiators also makes you look like you're desperately jumping onto the flavor of the month. For instance, if you say, "We're a cloud-based technology," so what? Every OS, application, and infrastructure solution is a potential cloud-based technology. Your message needs to outlast the latest craze.

One useful way to solve strategic messaging challenges is to think of your message in terms of "comprehensibility versus credibility." As Figure 5 shows, there is a continuum for messaging along both of these axes. A sweet spot exists for your message in terms of its credibility and comprehensibility. Simply put, you have four basic quadrants in which a message can land. At the top right, you have a clear and credible message. In this example, "Microsoft enters the smart phone business." Note that there are two big pillars on which this clear, credible message stands: The category is well understood and the company has the inherent brand credibility to make the claim. If the message were, "RinkyDinkComm enters the smart phone business," you would justifiably ask, "Who?" They lack credibility. Similarly, if the message were, "RinkyDinkComm, the leader in Cloud-Fusion Transactionality," you might ask both "Who?" and "What?"

Some messages are clear but hard to believe, such a company announcing it will overtake Google in search. I wish everyone the best of luck, but this is a mission that I cannot believe in right now. Going around the chart further, we have vague but credible, which is when a known brand stakes a claim in a poorly understood category. If you read "Microsoft, the leader in Cloud-Fusion Transactionality," you would probably think, "Well I don't have any idea what that is, but if Microsoft is doing it, it might be important!"

Certainly, there are no easy solutions for strategic messaging. This is a subjective, messy process, which involves a lot of trial and error. You will likely have to work at it for a while and repeat the creative process a number of times. Not everyone will be pleased with your strategic message, and in my experience trying to make all stakeholders happy is a sure-fire recipe for mediocrity.

CHAPTER 3: FILL THE PIPELINE

You will frequently hear sales and marketing people in the technology field talk about their "pipeline." What do they mean by the pipeline? Isn't a pipeline something which transports oil or gas from one place to another? Yes, a real pipeline is a large metal tube, often hundreds of miles long, through which oil or gas flows. The technology sales pipeline is a metaphor based on this idea. In the same way valuable oil flows out of the pipeline, so revenue flows out of the sales pipeline. So far, so good, but why the petroleum imagery?

Sales in the enterprise technology arena tend to be slow moving and complex to close. They also tend to be a rather big ticket. It might take a sales representative a year to close an enterprise technology deal, but the price tag could easily be over a million dollars.

Along the way, a lot of things can derail a deal from going through. To keep track of how their various deals are evolving, technology sales reps create a list of their pending transactions and rank them by stage of completeness. Sales automation tools, such as Salesforce.com, actually automate this process. The list of pending deals, or "deal flow" can be viewed as a future flow of revenue, as would oil flowing through the pipeline. A certain amount of revenue is expected to flow at certain points in the future.

A sales pipeline for an account executive selling enterprise might look like the one presented in Table 5:

Table 5 – Sample sales pipeline.

Opportunity	Stage	Amount	Probability	Expected Revenue	Age
Titan, Inc.	6 - Negotiation/Review	$ 67,000	90%	$ 60,300	200 days
Giant Corp.	5 - Verbal commitment	$ 240,000	70%	$ 168,000	100 days
Big Corp.	5 - Verbal commitment	$ 100,000	70%	$ 70,000	150 days
Teddy Bears Co.	4 - Pilot	$ 150,000	50%	$ 75,000	400 days
Googly Eyes	3 – Proposal/Price quote	$ 43,000	30%	$ 12,900	90 days
Whoopee Dolls	1 - Information gathering	$ 240,000	10%	$ 24,000	20 days
Action Figures, Inc.	1 - Information gathering	$ 140,000	10%	$ 14,000	10 days
Total		$ 980,000		$ 424,200	

This type of chart will look familiar to those of you who work with Salesforce.com. It is based on the opportunity forecast report. However, one need not have Salesforce.com automation software to create a pipeline report. A couple of comments on this chart:

- Business technology deals typically evolve through stages as they approach the close. Different sales organizations rank the stages in their own ways, but there is usually a progression from initial contact with the client through "closed." In this case, the company has created a scale, which looks something like this:

1. 10%-Information gathering
2. 20%-Prospect (ID'd Project, Budget, & PO)
3. 30%-Proposal/Price quote
4. 50%-Pilot
5. 70%-Verbal commitment

6. 90%-Negotiation/Review

7. 100% - Closed/Won

8. Closed/Lost

- What do the percentages mean? They have two functions in the sales pipeline. They help the sales rep, and his or her manager, understand how close the deal is to being done. A 10% opportunity has a long way to go and may easily fall out of the pipeline. For this reason, the percentage is also used to estimate projected revenue. This may sound a bit odd, but the standard practice is to multiply the gross value of the opportunity (i.e. how much money the deal will bring in) by the percentage of probability that the deal will close. For a $100,000 deal at a 10% stage of probability, it will be forecast on the pipeline as $10,000. You're probably thinking, why would you do that? The outcome will be either $100,000 or nothing, and this is in fact true. The deal will either come in or it won't. However, the percentages actually provide a good way of estimating how the rep is doing in terms of future sales. (The technique is borrowed from fancy math used to price oil futures and the like. It is called "decision theory" and is the bane of all first year MBA students.)

- The sales pipeline is thus valued in two ways. There is the gross dollar amount of the potential deals versus the projected probable revenue of those deals based on the stage percentages. A deal worth $100,000 with a 10% chance of closing, will show up as $10,000 on the pipeline. If a rep has a lot of big deals in the low percentage stages, these will show up as a low pipeline. The rep will then be aware that he or she has too many deals which are too far off in the future. The near term expected revenue will be low. As you can see, the percentages can be a useful tool for managing a sales rep's work.

- The pipeline is based on real business opportunities. In enterprise technology sales, nothing is real until a client has issued a purchase order. If you're dealing with small companies, you may have situations where someone makes a technology buy more or less on impulse or with little organized planning. This is not how it works in a big company. These companies only spend money on technology after everyone agrees the money should be spent, and this money exists in an approved budget. Often, there is a specific project ID number to connect the expenditure with the project. Until the project ID exists, there is no potential sale. Therefore, professional technology sales people should not put deals in their pipelines until they have some true commitment for a buy from the client. Of course, projects are cancelled and delayed, but deals should never be on the pipeline if they aren't legitimate. A project ID tells you that.

Before the Pipeline, the "Sales Funnel"

We're agreed, then - a deal does not belong in a sales representative's pipeline until it is a real revenue opportunity. This means that there is a customer planning to spend money on a specific type of solution. Talk is cheap in the sales pipeline; yet, for marketers, talk is a good start. Marketers are up for cheap talk, especially if it is with the right type of people. While sales people really only want to talk to people who have decided to buy, marketers are usually happy to chat with anyone who might buy our products.

Marketers, therefore, are interested in filling what is commonly known as the "Sales Funnel" depicted in Figure 6. The idea - a large volume of possible leads flow into the top of the funnel, but only qualified prospects drip out the bottom, ready to join the sales pipeline. The funnel metaphor is actually flawed. What we really mean is, this is a "sales filter," which eliminates the bad names and keeps the good.

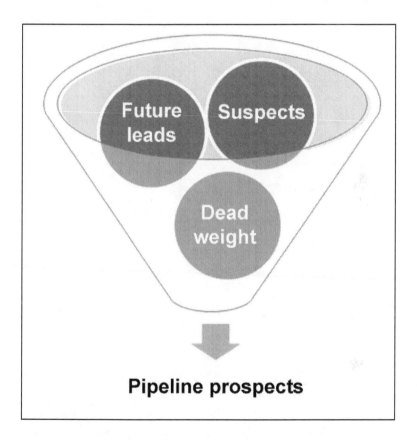

Figure 6 - The lead generation funnel.

The funnel, which consists of all manner of lead generation processes and events, catches a mixed multitude of potential pipeline prospects. Every marketer has a different way of categorizing these inbound leads, but the following labels are fairly standard:

- **Suspects** – People who may or may not be qualified to buy your product. More interaction is needed to make this determination.

- **Future leads** – People who are qualified to buy, but are not ready to buy. These people need to be nurtured until they are in the market for your product.

- **Dead weight** – People who are not qualified to buy, usually because they don't work for a company that needs your product. They are window shoppers, essentially. (Though, you never know… today's grad student researching a paper online is tomorrow's CTO!)

- **Pipeline prospects** – People who are qualified to buy and are in the market for your product.

Evaluating Sales Suspects

How do you know whether a suspect has the potential to be a real lead, which belongs in the pipeline? There are many different ways of making this distinction, though the most important takeaway from the discussion is that you, the marketer, must take responsibility for separating the lead generation wheat from the chaff. Your approach to differentiating promising leads from possible future prospects and unqualified dead weight will vary depending on several factors:

- **The price point of your product** – If you are selling a low cost product, you should be able to distinguish between buyers and non-buyers pretty easily. You can easily ask them if they want to buy or not. If they buy, great. If they don't, nurture them until they do. This can be accomplished over the phone or online through the use of an e-commerce site. More expensive products, which tend to require lengthy and deliberative purchasing decisions, need more intense qualification.

- **The nature of your sales cycle** – If your product has a long sales cycle, it will usually take more time and personal contact with the prospect to determine whether they are truly interested in buying. For example, in enterprise software, where deals can be in the millions of dollars, a true lead is someone who works at an entity which has already made a budgetary decision to buy the technology in question. In this case, a great lead-qualifying question might be, "Has your organization created a project and associated budget for this technology?" If the answer is "no" or "We're researching our options right now," this suspect is not qualified. Of course, the prospect may quickly become qualified, but as the marketer, you have to be aware of the distinction between a real lead and an information gatherer.

  Importantly, it is often most advantageous to become involved with the suspect at the early, information gathering stage. There is a risk that the opportunity will not pan out, but it is usually preferable to engage with the suspect before they have started to form strong views on the technology they are researching. At this stage, you can influence the way they think about things. Some sales people believe that once an RFP has been issued, you are too late. This is more true than you would believe. Many RFPs are written under the influence of (or even by) the top vendor candidate for the project. The other RFP respondents, who are at a huge disadvantage at this point, are merely solicited to show the buyer has "done his homework" and looked at alternatives to the anointed vendor. In sales terminology, this is known as being "column fodder." Smart sales people, and the marketers who support them, can smell column fodder situations and will refuse to bid in many cases.

- **The structure and process of your sales team** – If your lead generation process involves collecting names from typical sources such as your Website, trade shows, etc., and then simply turning them over to a sales representative, the rep is going to take care of qualifying the lead. For lower cost items (for the sake of argument, products which cost less than $5,000), the rep is generally the one who takes care of qualification. For higher ticket solutions, most technology companies have a two-tier sales force that qualifies new suspects before turning the real opportunities over to the senior sales people. What happens is that leads are transferred to an inside sales representative who calls the lead and asks a series of qualifying questions. Depending on the answers, the inside sales rep will decide to refer the lead up to the senior sales staff, relegate the lead to a future nurturing situation, or to the "unqualified" bin. Standard qualifying questions might include:

  o Are you planning to buy X? Yes/No

  o What is your timeframe for making the purchase?
    ▪ Now

- 3-6 months

- 6-12 months

- Don't know

o Does this purchase have budget allocated? Yes/No

o What is your role in the purchase process?

- Decision-maker

- Influencer

- Not involved

You might think, wow, those are pretty aggressive questions to ask someone who visited your Website or stopped by a tradeshow booth. Of course, there are more or less diplomatic and easygoing ways to ask these questions, but you must ask them. If you don't, you risk wasting your time and that of your sales team. Only the most qualified leads are deserving of account team time. A qualified lead has the following characteristics:

- Is definitely planning to buy

- Will be making a decision soon (i.e. Within 3 months)

- Has a budget

- Is a decision-maker or influencer

In other words, the prospect is ready to buy, has money, and can make (or influence) the buying decision.

• **Your level of marketing automation** – Teasing the qualification out of a prospect can be simple or challenging depending on the nature of what you're selling. For a complex, subjective, technology sale, it may take a number of conversations to clarify exactly what it is that the prospect actually needs. Is the prospect looking for a cloud-based email server, an email subscription service, an on-premise email server with a cloud option, or something else? If the prospect isn't sure what he or she wants, it will not be so easy to say "Yes, it's a qualified situation" or "No, it's not." For simple products, you can often easily ask a yes or no question online without ever having to speak with the prospect. You can see automated lead qualifications like this on many technology product sites. If you want to download a whitepaper and the site requires you to fill out an online form, the form will invariably ask you something like, "Are you planning to purchase XYZ in the next six months?" If you answer "no," you will be considered a second-class lead. (A majority of prospects probably want to be in this category because they don't want to hear a sales pitch. However, your material should be good enough where it intrigues the prospect and makes them want to hear more.) Some customer-resource management (CRM) and marketing automation tools such as HubSpot, enable you to set up fairly elaborate automated lead qualifying processes. These tools let you assign a numerical value to how each qualifying question on the form is answered. The results are totaled or run through a lead qualification scoring process. For instance, answering the question, "What is your purchase timeframe," might yield the following scores:

- Now = score of 10

- In 3-6 months = score of 7

- 6-12 months = score of 3

- 12+ months = score of 1

The system can then be programmed with lead assignment rules, which channel the high-scoring leads to account reps, while lower scoring leads remain unattended. You can create rule-based auto-response emails, which reply to form submissions depending on score. The prospect who receives a "10" for being ready to buy now gets the, "Someone will call you today" email, while a "1" gets the, "Thank you for your interest" reply. Generally, the higher the price and the longer the sales cycle, the more personal and complex the qualifying process will be.

Lead Generation Tension between Sales and Marketing

There is a great scene in *Glengarry Glen Ross* where Al Pacino chats up a potential client in a Chinese restaurant. The scene is a brilliant piece of theater, full of edginess and menace. As a marketer, though, I was most struck by the fact that Pacino played a salesman who developed his own leads. Oh, how rare this is!

Okay, I'll be nice. Lead generation can be a source of tension between sales and marketing groups. A lot of sales people believe that marketing is either not doing enough to generate leads, or is generating a lot of junk. Marketing, on the other side, claims they are generating plenty of names, but that the sales people aren't motivated or competent to follow up. What is the truth? The truth is somewhere in between.

One problem is that sales and marketing people have different views on what a "lead" actually is. For a salesperson, a lead is a well-qualified situation. In other words, a lead is someone who is ready to buy, has a budget, and is authorized to make the final decision. The salesperson's job is to show up, make the pitch, and bag the deal. As we know, these types of situations are hard to find.

For a marketer, a lead is someone who is generally qualified, meaning they are at a company which could afford to buy the product and they are in a role where they could influence the purchase decision. For example, if you're marketing security software for the enterprise, you consider a security manager at a Fortune 500 company to be a "lead." The salesperson might look at the same person and consider him or her the slightest of suspects, perhaps not even worth contacting. Who is right?

Both are right. Neither is right. Unfortunately, a deficit of leads as sales would define them can lead to acrimony between the sales and marketing teams. When the sales manager presses the reps on why they don't have bigger pipelines, the rep might say, "I'm doing the best I can, but marketing isn't getting me any leads." In turn, if asked, the marketing person might say, "Well, I sent the salesperson fifty names last week. What did he do with them?" In more situations than I would care to recall, the salesperson failed to call the leads marketing had generated. The salesperson's perspective, to be fair, is that the names may not be worth the salesperson's time. However, if he or she doesn't call, the qualification of the lead will forever remain a mystery. This is why many technology companies assign the task of calling all new leads to a designated inside sales representative.

One way to resolve this tension is through coordinated goal setting. As you have no doubt learned, finger-pointing feels good but solves nothing. My suggestion is for sales and marketing to sit down and work out an agreeable lead generation plan. Marketing needs to commit to generating a certain number or proportion of leads which the sales team would define as "qualified." This way, the marketing team has recognized sales' need for qualified leads. In turn, sales needs to commit to following up on every serious lead that the process creates. The plan would call for the generation of some gross number of "marketing leads," which may not be qualified enough to rate as "sales leads." If marketing cannot meet the plan objectives, then sales has a legitimate gripe. If marketing can "achieve plan," then sales needs to accept they have been given the number of leads they thought they needed to build a pipeline.

Filling the Pipeline – The Art of Demand Generation

Want to know how to fill the sales pipeline? Sorry, that is a trade secret. Send a big check, with an amount that looks like a phone number, except with a dollar sign in front of it, to me and I'll clue you in. No, I will be generous and give you what everyone wants to know: How to move sales leads into your pipeline. Known as "Lead Generation" or "Demand Generation," the process of attracting qualified prospects to your company and product offering is a bit of an art as well as a science.

First, the science. Lead generation should be a highly quantitative undertaking. You need to measure how you are doing or you will end up nowhere. Lead generation costs money. You want to know how much you are spending for every qualified lead which comes in. If you don't know how much you are spending, and which programs are working best (or not working), you will waste time and money.

Here is the art. Although lead generation is quantitative and analytical, it is still very much a creative marketing endeavor. You are constantly trying to figure out what magic mix of message and offer will grab a prospect's attention enough to stimulate a clear call to action, such as a sign-up or an enrollment in a Webcast. The art and science come together as you analyze different creative ideas and identify which ones are working and which are not. Then try to understand why and do better the next time around.

Inbound vs. Outbound Marketing

There are two basic modes of lead generation: Inbound and outbound. With inbound marketing, you set up mechanisms, such as Google ads and organic search rankings, and then wait for people to find you. Outbound lead generation involves more traditional forms of marketing, such as advertising, direct marketing, cold calling, and trade shows. Both forms of lead generation are useful and needed, though how you approach inbound and outbound, as well as the way you allocate resources to them, can have a big impact on the results you achieve.

Here is quick note about the term "inbound marketing." The growth of the Web and search engines has made the term "inbound marketing" synonymous with getting customers to engage with you over the Internet. However, I have also experienced a different use of the term, and this is worth clarifying. "Inbound marketing" can also refer to gathering "inbound" information about desired product features from customers and other stakeholders. In this context, inbound marketing relates to market research, focus groups, customer advisory boards, and so forth. The other term used to describe this activity is "product marketing." Some technology marketers work exclusively on product marketing, though at smaller companies a marketing generalist might also do product marketing duties along with many other tasks.

Some thoughts on the main types of inbound marketing:

This is far from an exhaustive list of inbound marketing techniques, but I wanted to give you quick rundown on the main ways technology companies use inbound marketing to generate leads. Entire books have been written about each category.

- **Website** – A great deal of Internet marketing focuses on helping people find your Website. It is easy to lose focus and forget that your Website itself has to be designed for lead generation. There are specialized practitioners who can design sites built for lead capture, though you can also do it yourself. Every page on your site should have some version of a call to action, or multiple calls. At very least, there should be a clickable "email us" link, but ideally each page should contain some offer – usually for content such as a whitepaper or video – which encourages the site visitor to register his or her information in exchange for the download. The navigation, design, and content of the site itself need to be oriented toward lead generation. It can't be excessive because this would turn people off. However, the thrust of the Website should be to encourage people to sign up for more information. The basic technique here is to provide a rich mass of freely accessible content to attract prospects to the site. Then, with the prospect engaged, the more enticing content is held "off limits" until the visitor registers.

- **Search Engine Optimization (SEO)** – SEO is a critically important topic, one that hundreds of experts, firms, and books address in great detail. Studies show that the purchase process in virtually 100% of technology acquisitions commence with a search engine, usually on Google! If your product doesn't appear in the top rankings (say, the first page or two of search results) you will be missing out big time on potential leads. Getting to the top of the rankings is a complex and labor-intensive process, but it is eminently doable and definitely profitable. There is a lot of nonsense floating around about secrets and hidden tricks to SEO, but it is wise to be very skeptical of such claims. Google's algorithm is secret, though a variety of techniques have been shown to achieve search results. The following is a far from exhaustive list of the established practices for SEO:

- **Link-building** – Google ranks search results by correlating the number of links to a site to its "authority" on a given subject. Before Google, search engines often returned a good deal of garbage in their results. One had to scroll through a lot of useless listings before finding something of value. Google's great genius was its realization that for any given search term, there were sites with "high authority." These high authority pages got to the top of the rankings. Authority is determined by many factors, but links from other sites count a great deal. The algorithm uses the linking site's authority as a factor in determining the authority of the linked-to page. Though the mechanics are secret, it's clear that Google assigns an authority score virtually every page on the Web. The higher the score of the linking site, the better you will be in SEO. If you can get nytimes.com, a very high authority site, to link to your site with reference for a term which is relevant to your business, this will be much more helpful in the search rankings than a link from a no-name source. A link to a site gets associated with a keyword through a process known as "anchor linking," where a URL is embedded in a term or phrase. Imagine you have an application server company called SoftCo, with the URL softco.com. If nytimes.com contains a hyperlink go your URL, softco, in an article, this is helpful. However, if nytimes.com contains the phrase "application server" with softco.com embedded in the text, this would be much better. That would associate the authority of nytimes.com with a link directly related to the target search term. An anchor link is done in html. It looks like this: <a href = "http://www.YOURURL.com">YOUR SEO TERM</a>. As you can imagine, linking involves reaching out to other entities, often through public relations and content creation, to build these important links. (They also known as "backlinks.") Some clever folks figured out that if they could generate hundreds of bogus Websites which link back to their site, it would help their rankings. This is known as "link farming" and the search engines are hip to the trick. Don't try it. Your search rankings will be deliberately forced lower as punishment.

- **On-page optimization** – The way the page is laid out can itself affect search results. Google and Bing use "Spiders," automated software that systemically "reads" your site to figure out which search terms match your content. The spiders "crawl" your site and examine the text on the page, the headlines you use, and other factors. If the SoftCo site includes the words "Application Server" written in the highest-level headline style of "H1", this will help emphasize that page's ranking for that term. Of course, if a million other sites also put the term in H1, the net effect on SEO is zero.

- **Content generation** – Search rankings are fluid. Your rank for a given term is bound to change as your competitors increase their optimization for this specific term. How can you keep up? One widely recommended approach, is to add a continual flow of new content to your site. Fresh content draws the attention of the search engines, which will periodically re-crawl and re-index your site. This re-crawling can help maintain or improve your search rankings. The most common way of adding this new content is by publishing a company blog rooted in your site's URL. Thus, for www.softco.com, the blog should be blog.softco.com. Regular posts will trigger interest from the search engine crawlers. Of course, the content has to be good, and it has to reference your targeted keywords. There is a delicate balance to strike with content creation, however. You cannot simply stuff your blog posts with repetitions of keywords. The major search engines are extremely sophisticated in their ability to sniff out tricks of this type. If your blog posts are deemed to be a ruse, you will be punished in the rankings.

- **Momentum and consistency** – The search engines allegedly reward momentum and consistency in Web presence. A site which has been live for 10 years enjoys a ranking advantage over a new site. A site that is updated with fresh content, such as blog posts, on a regular basis, will get a ranking advantage over a competing site that is static for the equivalent period of time.

- **URLs** – This may seem obvious, but search terms contained directly in a site's URL are helpful to search engine rankings.

As with so many other elements of SEO, it is very difficult to determine just how much advantage having a search-friendly URL will be, but it definitely helps. If SoftCo uses appserver.com it would be more useful in search results than softco.com. You can also add search terms to a URL, so softco.com becomes softco.com/application_server. According to SEO experts, this addition helps, but is less powerful than having the root URL contain the search term.

• **Metadata** – Each Web page contains metadata. Metadata is information (data) that describes other data. This document itself contains both. It has the text you are reading right now. That is the data. The metadata, which you cannot see, contains facts such as the font I am using or the size of the font. With Web pages, metadata describes what is on the page. It is possible to add search terms to a page's metadata, or "meta tags." Keywords in metadata are allegedly helpful, but the consensus among SEO experts is that meta tags are not as effective at pushing a site up in the rankings as the used to be. Like many other facets of Web design for SEO, keyword meta tags are subject to abuse, which the search engines penalize.

The effectiveness of the many SEO techniques ebbs and flows as the algorithms change over time. However, this does not mean someone has the magic key to it all. (And, dear reader, for some strange reason, that person always wants to charge a huge fortune for the secret.) No, the basics of SEO are well proven to work, and they are not secret. They are, however, somewhat difficult to execute effectively, given the massive range of possible keywords, meanings, interpretations, and competitive factors on the Web.

SEO is always challenging, but it is somewhat simpler when you are in a clear-cut consumer product category, which is seldom the case in technology marketing. If you sold auto insurance, the keywords you want to rank on would include "auto insurance," "car insurance" and close correlates of those terms. In technology marketing, things are never that clear. Imagine SoftCo is considering developing an image repository application with a photo management portal. The company investigates which keywords might be the most effective for optimization. That is, when potential buyers of the SoftCo photo product search for a solution, which keywords will they use? Which are the most relevant words for which SoftCo should optimize in order to capture the greatest number of qualified buyers through the search process?

If you enter the term "Enterprise Photo Portal" into the Google Keyword Tool, Google tells you there are, in fact, no searches for the term at all, as shown in the table below. For related terms, shown further down in the table, the keyword tool gives you data on how competitive the term is, as well as monthly searches for the term and estimated cost-per-lick (CPC). If SoftCo wanted to optimize for "Enterprise Portal," it would be potentially surfacing in 33,100 searches per month. The competition is .2, which means that the term has relatively little competition. The higher the competition number, the harder it is to rank high in search results. In contrast, the term "Portal Software" has a competition grade of .69, which indicates many more Websites are trying to rank high in search results for that term.

Table 6 – Example of keyword competition and search volume for SEO.

Keyword	Competition	Global Monthly Searches	Local Monthly Searches	Estimated Avg. Cost Per Click (CPC)
enterprise photo portal	-	-	-	$0.05
enterprise portal	0.2	33,100	9,900	$5.21
enterprise portals	0.2	33,100	12,100	$5.24
portal software	0.69	22,200	8,100	$4.54
portal integration	0.13	3,600	1,000	$4.98
portals company	0.67	320	170	$5.26
enterprise portal strategy	0.3	91	46	$0.05
portal enterprise	0.2	33,100	9,900	$0.00
portals software	0.69	22,200	8,100	$0.05

One of the main principles of SEO is to optimize for keywords which have relatively high search volume but low competition. In the example shown in Table 6, the phrase "Enterprise Portal" is superior to "Portal Software." It will take much more work and investment to get SoftCo to the top of the search rankings for "Portal Software." But, here is the rub: SEO is about more than just ranking in the search results. You have to rank amongst searches by the right type of prospect. If you get a high rank for a term which is used by people who won't buy your product, you will not have accomplished much.

- **Pay per click advertising / Search engine marketing** - Those green text boxes you see on the right when you conduct a Google search are paid ads matched to the keyword that is being searched. The advertiser pays nothing until a searcher clicks on the link. This is known as "Pay Per Click" or "PPC" advertising. If SoftCo wanted to buy advertising on Google for the term "Enterprise Portal," they would pay about $5.21 for each person who clicked on their ad. This might be a lot or a little, depending on your rate of conversion. PPC advertising is very tricky and it is quite easy to waste money if you are not careful. However, it can be a great solution if you manage it well. You can short circuit the laborious and uncertain terrain of natural SEO. SEO can take months. PPC is instant.

- **Directories** – For almost every product category, there is a directory which points prospective buyers to vendors. You want to be listed in as many directories as possible, though be careful about overblown paid listings. Directories exist in both print and online forms. Both are viable and should be examined for potential inbound marketing potential. It is tempting to dismiss print in the digital era, but it is worth checking to see whether people in your industry segment still refer to print directories. Chances are, there is at least one trusted print directory – often a special issue of a well-known industry magazine – that prospects keep on their book shelves and refer to when they are thinking about buying something. Many online directories are free, or may actually be someone's blog. These informal listings are often the best as they potentially embody the highly sought-after quality of neutral third-party opinion.

- **Extended online reach** – Prospects have to be able to find you, even when they are not searching for you. Your inbound marketing plan should address your need to have an extended presence online. This may blur with search engine and social media activities, but you want your name and URL appearing in as many relevant online locations as possible.

Closed Loop Marketing

The process of generating inbound leads and then cultivating them until they become real prospects is known as "closed loop marketing." This is similar to stocking a pond with fish. It is a lot easier to catch a fish if you keep them trapped in an enclosed space. The alternative, which is hanging your line in a pond with an unknown quantity of fish, can be a lot less effective. So it is with sales leads. Once you have attracted a suspect to your product and put them in this enclosed space – or "loop," you can work on them inside this closed loop until they become a revenue source.

There is a whole art to this iteration of lead nurturing. Like so many other marketing activities, lead nurturing is about finding the right balance between persistence and annoyance. If a suspect immediately pops up and becomes a real sales lead, wonderful! For the other 99.9% of leads you put into your closed loop inbound marketing process, you will need to work gently on pushing them over the finish line. Some marketers send newsletters or follow-up emails, or call, and it all works if you do it with some subtlety.

Automated follow-up, as performed by closed loop marketing solutions such as Marketo and others, is sometimes referred to as "drip campaigning." Once the prospect has registered, the automated closed loop marketing system starts to "drip" follow-up messages and new content offers over a period of time. For instance, you might receive an instant thank you email once you register for a paper. A week later, you'll be invited to watch a pre-recorded Webinar. A week after, you'll be asked whether you want a live demo. In many cases, these follow up emails are automatically generated.

It can be easy to overdo it with lead cultivation. Imagine you are some hapless IT person who needs information about a product. You download a white paper and the next thing you know, you're receiving an email a week from a company you've barely heard of. Good or bad? It depends.

If those emails have valuable information in them, the prospect may start to associate your brand with value and usefulness. If irritating sales pitches are showering down on him or her, you are going to suffer. I still receive emails from companies for which I've long since forgotten the original reason I contacted them. I can't even remember who they are or what they do. I call this "spamnesia." It is annoying and counterproductive.

One consequence of the closed loop phenomenon, which has really taken off in the last five years or so, is that prospects are becoming a lot more hip to the tricks of lead cultivation. People know they are going to be bombarded with junk if they register for your site. I am seeing a trend where leads sign up for marketing materials with fake email addresses or Gmail accounts. These accounts never get read. Some inbound marketing tools enable you to block phony registrations or public email accounts. The takeaway is still the same, though, from a marketing perspective. If you offer valuable content and information, people will take you seriously. If you're spamming them, you'll get what you deserve.

One additional comment on inbound marketing: In general, gimmicks don't work. We have all heard of some super clever concept for capturing leads. There is usually some breathless story about an Android app which simulates a ski jump and gets people to register for a software demo. I am sure such tricks work sometimes, but most of these success stories are from consumer marketing. This is another area where consumer and B2B technology marketing diverge, in my experience.

Outbound Marketing

I am not going to dwell on outbound marketing as it involves techniques most of us know well. Briefly, outbound marketing includes activities which push your message out to various audiences with the hope that the recipients will react by volunteering to enter your closed loop. In this way, outbound and inbound marketing are really two parts of the same process.

This will not be true if you are marketing a product which can be purchased at a store or through a reselling partner. In these cases, your outbound efforts will be prompting the audience to take an action apart from your closed loop. In enterprise technology, however, you are almost always encouraging prospects to sign up as leads, through outbound marketing.

The following are the primary types of outbound marketing for a technology company:

- **Advertising** – Including display advertising in magazines, outdoor, and mass media. Advertising is a big company game. The focus is about branding, and companies such as IBM and Oracle are great examples of the brand value of persistent advertising. After hundreds of exposures to their messages, you have internalized the concept that IBM and Oracle get what your business is all about. That level of exposure is not cheap. Advertising takes big bucks, and I don't recommend it for startups. Yes, there is some value in establishing a known brand in print, perhaps in specialized trade publications, but in my experience it is seldom the best use of marketing dollars in the early stages.

- **Direct marketing** – Marketing technology products involves connecting with decision-makers. Direct marketing is a great way to accomplish this goal. Direct (USPS) mail, email marketing, and cold-calling are all examples of direct marketing. Three main challenges arise with direct marketing, however, and the best technology marketers are constantly trying to stay on top of their game when it comes to the following:

  o **Staying on message** – Marketing the latest technology

is a process which, by definition, tends to be a bit vague. Holding with my view that if you can truly nail your category and message, you're too late, you will be creating some direct marketing pieces with messaging which is guaranteed to confuse at least a few people. My recommendation is to focus on clear value and worry less about categorizing yourself. SoftCo could waste a lot of time and mix up a lot of prospects by messaging about its features as "Photo Portal" or a "Content Manager." Instead, they should concentrate on how their product saves time and money for information workers.

o **Creating a compelling call to action** – If you think about the way you react to direct marketing attempts to get your attention, you will understand that your prospects will spend about one second deciding whether or not your message and offer are worth their time. We need to be super harsh on ourselves about this. Direct marketing is not a domain for wishful thinking. Direct marketing is about grabbing the prospect's attention and triggering a desired action. If the messaging is off or the call to action is not interesting, they will pass you by. Consider the difference in impact between offering a sales demo versus a free white paper on a topic of interest to the prospect. The white paper is probably going to create more interest because it's informative without being overtly sales-oriented.

o **Getting through** – One of the most basic challenges to success in direct marketing is simply getting through to your target recipient at all. Thanks to all the boring, annoying, and unethical direct marketers out there (this would be everyone except you and me, of course!), people have erected vast defenses against the invasion of direct marketing messages. Phone calls go to voice mail. Mail is tossed by assistants. Email goes to spam... How can you get through? The truth: It is not easy, but it is possible. Some thoughts:

o **Follow email best practices,** e.g., don't use terms like "free offer" in your message, which will flag it as spam.

o **Design direct mail pieces which are striking and have explicit messaging on the outside -** e.g., don't expect people to open a plain envelope in order to get to your marketing message.

o **Pursue diligent, high quality calling processes** – Cold calling can work if you've planned correctly. It takes a lot of work and professionalism, but you can make an impact on people over the phone if you are persistent and know what to say when they do pick up.

There are numerous online resources that can help you structure high-impact direct marketing campaigns, as well as agencies that specialized in getting through.

- **Shows** – Trade shows and conferences are a staple of outbound marketing for technology companies. We've all done (one too many of) them in our careers. Shows are seductive, in that you can effortlessly meet all kinds of prospects. They've intentionally travelled to the show. You are there. This is a perfect fit. There are no irritating calls or emails to interrupt their day. And, it can work.

  It is essential that you carefully track your results from trade shows. Many trade show leads are not high quality, even if they are from major potential buyers. Again, message and offer are important here. If you meet a lead at a tradeshow and hand them an imprinted pen before scanning their badge, you have not accomplished much. If you can engage the prospect in a discussion about how your solution is relevant to his specific business problems, you may be on first base. One thing to be aware of is that certain venues (I'm referring here to New York City) are notorious for allowing people off the street into trade show halls to give the appearance of foot traffic. I've seen this numerous times, mostly in New York, where all manner of whacked out people will appear at the booth claiming to be "consultants" but are really there just to abscond with promotional freebies.

- **Webcasts and live events** – Convincing people to show up in person for a live marketing event is getting more and more difficult to accomplish. Until about 2000, fancy breakfast presentations in New York and the Bay Area were *de rigueur* for enterprise technology marketing. Today, it is much more common to assemble a group of prospects for an online presentation. The impact may be lower but the attendance and costs are significantly more attractive. Some event companies offer exclusive retreats and summits with senior IT executives. In my experience, these can be quite effective, though they are extremely costly. You have to figure out whether your product is ready enough and your fit with the buyer is good enough to part with $40,000 plus in exchange for a dozen or more face to face meetings. But, bear in mind - **you may never get face time with these buyers any other way**.

A couple of "Have to's" in outbound marketing: You have to know which way the wind is blowing as it relates to the outbound techniques you select. Every approach to outbound marketing has its weak points, and some audiences are less receptive to specific forms of communication than others. You need to be sensitive to what works and what doesn't. And, this changes over time. In the last few years, we've seen a big decline in the effectiveness of email marketing blasts, even when it is done with carefully selected "opt-in" lists. Believe it or not, I have seen situations where a return to the old tried-and-true cold calling technique is more effective than electronic outreach.

The way you know if a technique is working is by tracking your results. This is the other "have to" in outbound marketing. It is absolutely imperative that you keep track of how your outbound marketing is working. If you are doing email advertising, for example, you need to keep track of the response rates to each list. Then, as leads enter your sales funnel from the email campaigns, you should track how they fare. It is tempting to become excited when you get a high click-through rate, but if the people who click through are junk leads, then you haven't accomplished much. It may take months to follow leads as they make their way through the sales process. As you retroactively gather data on the effectiveness of different campaigns and techniques, you should adjust your tactics moving forward.

Chapter 4: Create Preference

It may sound duplicative single out creating preference as a specific area of technology marketing. All marketing is about creating preference. Everything you do is meant to drive preference of your product over others. Yet, it helps to be aware of the mandate to create preference as you go about your marketing work. Preference building has its own specific tasks and challenges. Plus, it is so basic that it actually gets overlooked fairly often.

For One Thing, It's About the Product

One basic starting point: <u>The product itself matters</u>. We marketers can become so caught up in our messaging, campaigns, and hype building that we become out-of-touch with the very product we are promoting. The 2011 demise of the Flip Video Camera can teach us a bit about this phenomenon. I do not know personally what went on inside Cisco, which drove their decision to drop the product entirely, but I do know that the Flip Cam got overtaken by the smart phone as a video device. It became harder to sell the consumer on a dedicated video camera when so many smart phones contained a comparable and sometimes superior-performing feature. The target customer groups for the Flip Cam and the smart phone are similar, so this buyer is probably going to go with a video-equipped phone rather than two devices, even if the Flip had better video quality. No amount of clever marketing in the world was going to shift this preference.

The Product Preference Flow

Let's refresh on the overall flow of preference that we want to drive. Before we can close a sale, our prospect has to go through some version of the following flow of events:

1. Awareness – The prospect is aware that your company and your product exist.

2. Consideration – The prospect considers your product as a potential solution for their business need.

3. Preference – The prospect prefers your product over other competing products.

4. Selection – The prospect selects your product over competitors and purchases it.

Each stage of the preference flow involves different aspects of marketing, and to some extent, sales. Table 7 summarizes the key marketing activities that go with each stage of the preference flow.

Table 7 – The product preference stages, from awareness through selection, and related marketing activities.

Stage	Key marketing activities
Awareness	Advertising, lead generation activities, public relations, social media, Website
Consideration	Website, datasheets, battle cards and other collateral, case studies
Preference	Proposal support, whitepapers, analyst relations
Selection	Sales support

As the process flows from awareness to preference and selection, marketing's role diminishes. Figure 7 below shows how the emphasis from market to sales shifts over the course of the preference process. The work of convincing a specific prospect to select a product over your competitor's, is the responsibility of sales. Of course, sales needs marketing's help to make its case for preference and selection.

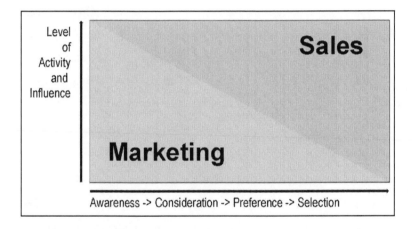

Figure 7 - Contrasting the roles of sales and marketing as the customer gets closer to actual product selection.

Mapping the Mind of the Customer

When we talk about building preference, we are really talking about shifting the prospect's inner mindset about our product. We have to become mind-readers and then mind-changers, in this process. This may seem like a tall order. How can we know what is on the prospect's mind? (As Eddie

Murphy did so well in *Trading Places*, he knew that the pork belly buyer was anxious to buy his son the GI Joe with the Kung Fu Grip!) Well, we can't know what is truly on the prospect's mind, but we can make some fairly accurate guesses.

Think about it like this: If you see a man standing in the cold without a jacket on, you can read his mind. He is thinking, "I'm cold." He might also be thinking, "I'm angry at life," but that is beyond our marketing mind-reading abilities. When a prospect is considering your product, there is more on their mind than "I need X-type of product." What is on the mind of a prospective SoftCo buyer? He needs a photo portal of some type. That is a given. If he didn't need one, you wouldn't be interested in talking to him. But, what is **really** on his mind? Let's do some mind-reading.

Reading the prospect's mind is partly dependent on his or her job role. IT people tend think differently from business managers though a lot of their respective issues are similar. The mind of the prospect is usually filled with three competing forces, as depicted in the preference pyramid show in Figure 8. Let's break them down and understand how the tug-of-war in the prospects mind can affect the preference process:

- **Needs** – What the prospect needs should be fairly simple to pin down, though not always. Even if the prospect doesn't know the precise product he needs, he usually understands what he wants the end solution to do. In this case, it would be a portal which could manage images for an enterprise behind the firewall.

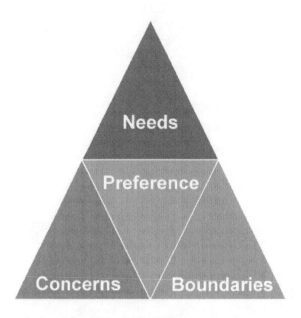

Figure 8 - The preference pyramid.

- **Concerns** – Working in the opposite direction are concerns about things which may go wrong with the vendor or solution. Concerns abound, but a few notable ones include the following:

    o Will this product work as advertised?

    - Do these people know what they are doing?

    - Is this product good enough?

    o Will the vendor support it the way I need them to?

    o Is the product developed with the right type of technology? Will it become obsolete?

o Will the vendor go out of business or be acquired by a company we don't like?

o Will the product cause problems elsewhere in our IT ecosystem, in the form of excess network load, software integration hassles, or disruptions in existing processes?

o Are there hidden costs, such as dependent licenses, that we are not aware of?

o Will we be "locked in" to this vendor and have a costly problem if we want to change direction down the road?

- **Boundaries** – Pushing back against needs and concerns are boundaries which limit the purchasing options. Here are some major boundaries that you may run into:

  o We are a Microsoft/IBM/Oracle/SAP shop. We will never buy a product not made by that vendor or certified to work with it.

  o We only host applications on premise. We never use "the cloud."

  o The solution we choose must work with Mac, Windows, Linux, Android, and so on – we will never choose something which doesn't work on these platforms.

o   Cost – let's not forget this one, because this is quite basic. Some of the best solutions are priced right out of the buyer's budget.

Now, with this pyramid in mind, think about the product you are taking to market. How will the buyer perceive your offering given the three competing forces going on in his or her mind? Will concerns outweigh needs or drive the buyer to an alternative vendor? Will boundary issues force the buyer out of considering your product or inhibit preference?

What is the single most important element, which can tip the preference thought process in your favor? Excluding bribery, the number one quality to have in your prospect's mind is confidence. *Confidence.* Let's say it again: Confidence. To position yourself as "preferred" in the mind of the prospect, you need to instill confidence in your product. To illustrate the principle of confidence in enterprise technology marketing, consider Table 8, which shows how an IT manager might think about two similar products, one from IBM and the other from a lesser-known vendor.

Table 8 – Issues affecting preference.

Issue affecting preference	Perception of IBM	Perception of IBM Competitor
Long-term support	IBM supports all products for a minimum of five years.	Vendor is unclear about length of support.
Customization	IBM can provide virtually limitless professional services resources for customization.	Vendor has a small professional services team that may or may not be able to handle customization demands.
Mainframe integration	Solid as a rock.	Vendor has a mainframe plug in.
Scalability	The IBM product is built on the WebSphere platform, which has proven scalability.	The vendor's product is J2EE based and scales well in theory.

How much more confidence will the IT manager have in the IBM solution? Probably a lot more. Confidence is one of the reasons why IBM is so successful. Their track record, culture, and depth of resources instill a great deal of confidence amongst potential buyers. Thus, we have the classic saying, "No one ever got fired for buying IBM." Of course, they don't win every deal, but when they lose, it will likely be due to confidence issues flowing in the other direction. Smaller vendors can engender confidence that they will work harder to please the client than a giant like IBM. Or, the smaller vendor will build confidence by their giving the client the best value. In this subject, I am indebted to Donald Cooper, a business thinker whose work has been a source of inspiration for me for many years.

Human Marketing – The Four Currencies

Donald Cooper is a successful entrepreneur and speaker who approaches marketing from the perspective of satisfying human needs. He calls it "Human Marketing," and at its essence, it is about instilling preference through confidence. Cooper talks about the *"four currencies,"* which we all use in our lives and business.

- Money

- Time

- Feeling safe (physically & emotionally safe)

- Feeling special

In Cooper's view, people are constantly searching for **more** of these *"four currencies."* Note that money is just one "currency." Money is not the only arbiter of preference. As Cooper puts it, "People are prepared to spend more money to save time, or to feel safer, or more special. Think about your own life. People are even prepared to take time and to spend a lot of money to <u>not</u> feel safe, in order to feel special...which is the only explanation I have for bungee jumping!"

I see Cooper's theory manifesting itself in many aspects of technology marketing. IT buyers will spend money on technologies which help them save time (easier to maintain, fewer problems), make them feel safe (in terms of job security and stress), and make them feel special. Yes, this last one is a bit funny, but it is more true than any of us could imagine. IT people want to feel special, just like the rest of us. In the case of enterprise technology, feeling special might come from achieving a level of CPU utilization no one else thought possible, or some other esoteric, yet important aspect of IT.

Confidence is the *one* underlying factor which drives all of this. The buyer will prefer and select the product which engenders confidence. The product will provide the greatest amount of these four currencies. Our approach to building preference should therefore be informed by the following ideas:

- Our product saves you money or helps you make more of it.

- With our product, you will have more time on your hands to do what you really want to do.

- You can feel safe (in your job) and secure (you won't get yelled at) and stress free.

- Our product will make you feel special, giving you all types of unique technology bragging rights.

These four ideas are typically in the subtext of any well-crafted messaging for a technology product. In some cases the message is overt, though in a lot of cases it is implicit. The goal is always the same - build preference by instilling confidence that this product will deliver on these four critical currencies.

Levers of Preference

Everything in marketing should drive preference. Preference is inherent in the product itself, and all marketing is oriented toward building preference over competitors. Every piece of marketing copy needs to play on the reader's desire to accumulate the *"four currencies."* This can be a stealth mission with subtle and indirect gestures pushing the reader to consider how your product will give him or her a newfound wealth of money, time, and security. A few specific marketing activities, however, should be pursued distinctly with preference in mind.

- **Demos** - A demonstration of your product has to be jammed with calls for preference, even if they are subtle. Everything said in a demo is prefaced by the unsaid, "Compared to everyone else, we do…" How can you frame your demo to make the statement sound like, "Compared to everyone else, we are better, because of xyz?" The SoftCo photo portal offers better security features than its competitors. It integrates with all the leading identity management systems, while the competitors only integrate with one ID system. The "feature barfing" approach to showcasing this advantage is to say, "We integrate with all identify management systems." There is no harm in saying it this way, but it would be a lot more effective in terms of preference building if the advantage were stated along the lines of, "You don't have to worry about integrating with your identity management system." This latter approach emphasizes the true advantage of the SoftCo product in human marketing terms.

- **Public relations** – PR is the first of three work areas which can drive confidence and preference. Similar to the other two, analyst relations and case studies, PR is all about showing off neutral third parties, which have good things to say about your product. In PR, your goal is to get reporters, and increasingly bloggers and other hybrid personalities to write about your product. The PR field has changed radically in the last five years. Paper and ink clippings used to be the ultimate goal. Today, links to online articles are everything. While an article in a print magazine is nice, it is actually most useful as a shareable online PDF. The end goal has remained the same, however, which is to get other people to talk about how great your product is and build preference through the confidence it instills. Media mentions take several forms, each of which is helpful. However, "not all PR is created equal."

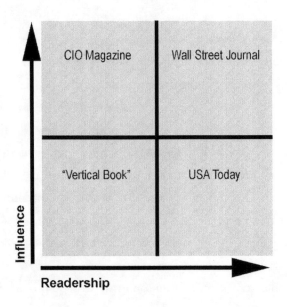

Figure 9 - Measuring the true impact of public relations - influence vs. readership.

- Which is worth more, a thousand words in an industry vertical publication or 200 words in the Wall Street Journal? It depends, of course on what you are trying to accomplish, but in general, the more influential the publication and the greater its readership, the more helpful the "ink" is going to be in driving preference and confidence. A positive mention in the *Wall Street Journal* instills confidence. A feature article in the *Wall Street Journal* is golden, assuming it is saying something good about you. Figure 9 depicts this tradeoff between readership and influence. The old adage, "I don't care what you say about me - just spell my name correctly," doesn't apply to technology PR and confidence-building. A negative product review will probably hurt you more than being omitted from the review altogether.

- **Analyst relations** – Reports by recognized industry analysts can have a huge impact on preference and confidence. Analysts offer themselves to the market as the ultimate in third parties. They are neutral and knowledgeable. They compare products and select top candidates for consideration. The result, as you already may know, is that analysts can command serious dollars for their work. To be sure, analyst relations is a subtle game with many misconceptions and myths surrounding it.

  o There are two classes of analysts. A small, select group is paid by enterprise buyers for their opinions. The biggest of course is Gartner, though Forrester and some specialized smaller firms also belong to this elite group. Other analyst firms are able to offer market insights to vendors and publish reports which are of general interest. However, they are not viewed as being completely impartial by the buyer.

  o You cannot buy good analyst coverage. The myth is that you have to "pay off" the good analysts in order to receive positive coverage. This is not entirely true. What is true, though, is that if you are not a client of the analyst firm, you will likely not get much attention from them. And, there is some truth to the idea that you pay to engage with the analyst firm to the point where your products and views better known to them than if you did not engage with them. In other words, if you invite analysts to visit you for consulting, they will have much more exposure to you than if you didn't. But it will cost you. At the end of the process you will still receive an honest review, which you will listen to if you are smart.

- **Case studies** – True accounts of real customers using your product are a fantastic way to move the needle on preference and confidence. Buyers like to see their industry peers using your product before they will entrust you with their business. No brainer, right? Well… Case studies are not hard to create. Typically, you interview the customer and write a two-page document which summarizes the business challenge that the customer faced and how they solved it with your product. So far, so good. The problem arises with obtaining permission. Small companies generally don't mind being the subject of a case study. In fact, they might feel flattered and enjoy the publicity. Big companies, especially those that are publicly traded, dislike having their names used (or misused, as they might put it) by vendors. Big companies are quite reluctant to grant you permission to publish a case study about them. Their reluctance is based partly on a concern about brand dilution as well as possible liability. If Coke allows a vendor to use its name, and the vendor is later accused of fraud, that might reflect badly on Coke. In general, if you are willing to grant favors or discounts to the client, you may be able to buy a case study from a big client.

Chapter 5: Understand the Industry and the Market

U nderstanding the market you are in may seem so obvious, it doesn't bear discussion in a book about marketing. However, in technology marketing, especially in the enterprise segment, the industry is so continually in flux, it can be nearly impossible to pin down your category. This is particularly true for newer technologies.

Streaming Video vs. UC

I've recently been immersed in some confusion about categorization confusion surrounding webcasting and video streaming. Where do they fit in the technology industry? An easy answer is within the "enterprise video" marketplace, which is described as an approximately $700 million year segment. You could also make a pretty good argument that enterprise video streaming is part of the much larger "Unified Communications" (UC) sector. UC used to describe everything from phone handsets to video chat applications. UC is a potentially massive category, encompassing much of what is now thought of as the phone industry – a hundred billion dollar plus space! Or, is online video for corporations actually part of "Unified Communications and Collaboration" (UCC)? Which is it - and does it matter?

Here is a deceptively simple question: Do you need to know what market you are in if you are going to sell a product? Maybe yes. Maybe no. It is always shocking to me how many technology marketers are unable to fill in the blanks of, "This is my product. It is a _____ product that does _____." When I worked on the Microsoft SharePoint team, there was little definitive agreement on what type of product it was, even though it was selling at a rate of over a billion dollars a year. It was a collaboration tool, a content manager, a search engine and a Web authoring environment. It was almost a foot cream.

Think about the evolution of cell phones into smart phones, which is now evolving yet again into the split between phones, smart phones and app-phones, and tablets. You could easily choose to buy a device without caring about whether it would be an app-phone or a smart phone. You might have chosen the device because it had features and functions which you liked. Perhaps it was a good value?

With corporate technology we don't see much of a difference. If you are considering a voice-over-IP (VOIP) system, how much impact will the product's categorization have on you? If the product is part of the UCC category, rather than just regular UC, will it matter? At a feature level, whichever product fits your needs best should be the choice. You may instead be influenced by analysts who report on product segments, regarding what they think the future holds and what it will mean for your product selection. If you read, "collaboration solutions will inevitably merge with communications, making UCC triumphant over basic UC," it may influence your selection.

The real reason categories matter is because they tell people a lot about how certain vendors are doing. Product categorization and market segmentation in the technology industry is mostly about the vendors. Who is winning? Who is not? This is the source of the confusion. Vendors want, for many reasons, to be perceived as the winner in the marketplace. Who wouldn't, right? But, the preoccupation with being the winner leads to some awful marketing problems. Vendors face pressure to categorize their offerings as winners, even if the winning segment isn't well defined. Thus, we end up saying, "This is my [*winningest, cutting edgiest*] product," not "This is my [well known, reliable but low cost] product."

Valuation is the biggest driver of categorization confusion. Venture capitalists and the stock market place quite different values on technology companies based on their perception of what they are doing and how they are doing. This is only fair and reasonable. All businesses are valued based on their perceived potential to generate future earnings. However, in the technology business, the valuation dynamics can be a bit out of sync with reality. Tech is one of the few business sectors where people can realize massive gains in valuation based largely on what Wall Street folks call "deal optics" – what you *look* like you're doing. We have gone through several cycles of boom and bust over this, with a few long-term performers, such as Apple, eBay, and Microsoft still on the market. Even after the "tech wreck" of 2002, when so many vaporous technology companies imploded, the market still has an appetite for the next big thing.

Categorization is directly tied to valuation. If you are in the enterprise software field, one dollar of revenue for your product deployed as a traditional on-premise server solution will translate into about $2 of entity valuation. A dollar of revenue of your product deployed as a software-as-a-service (SaaS) or cloud solution will give you $6 of valuation. If you are doing $10 million in on-premise business, you're worth $20 million. If you're doing $10 million in SaaS, you're worth $60 million! What would you rather have?

As a result of these types of valuation practices, technology companies engage in egregious contortions to categorize themselves in the high value fields. In this way, a maker of mainframe tools becomes "an SOA infrastructure player," an email service becomes a "cloud-based collaboration company," and so on. I have come up with a joke to describe this challenge. I say, "If you can accurately define what category you are in, you are too late." From a valuation perspective, the interesting stuff in the technology market is happening where things are fast moving and loosely defined.

To be fair, the customer is not always confused by valuation-driven category blurring. Some enterprise buyers want the latest thing. And, in a lot of cases, the latest thing is what they really need. Budget constraints might push a sincere interest in migrating systems to the cloud. Thus, even though cloud computing might be the *"flavor du jour,"* and derided as a fad, this is a real technology with strong benefits for the right buyer. Where things become murky is when technologies try to dress themselves up to be something they are not. This benefits no one.

In the case of enterprise video, if I define myself as being in the enterprise video category I'm limiting myself to a small market with limited upside. (I realize $700M seems like a lot of money, but for a venture capitalist trying to arrange a big exit, this is chicken feed.) Yet, it is the closest category to what a corporate video product really does. If I put myself into the much larger UC category, I'm not being clear about what my product actually does. The VCs will be happy, but my customers will be confused. The chart below shows how I attempted to categorize enterprise webcasting software.

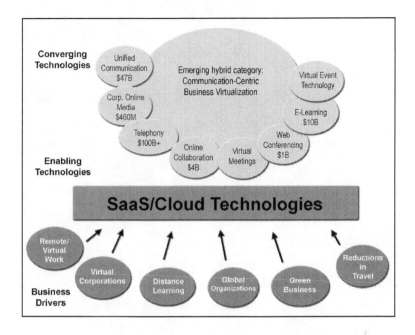

Figure 10 - The "Abstractagon" of industry definition and sizing

Figure 10 is what I call an *"abstractagon,"* a visual crime committed in the name of helping technology entrepreneurs find clarity in their strategy. In this case, I am trying to show how the relatively small category of enterprise video fits into an evolving landscape of online communication and business virtualization. The idea was to situate the product accurately in the small category but show how enterprise video was morphing into something bigger. Business drivers such as remote work and virtual corporations, combined with the distance learning and green businesses trends were creating opportunities for new technologies like UCC and virtual meetings. Video was a factor in many of these new technologies, so it was possible to identify places were the small enterprise video category would grow as it merged with others.

If you are confused about what market you are in, one approach is to look at the major vendors and see what they are doing and with whom they are partnering. Microsoft describes SharePoint as a collaboration tool, among other things. Their site says, "Microsoft SharePoint 2010 makes it easier for people to work together." This tells you that the idea of collaboration tools is going to be gaining traction in the marketplace, or at least in buyer-vendor conversations. Why should you care what Microsoft is doing? Well, the reality is, a big vendor such as Microsoft is going to be heard when it talks about its product categories. When I was public relations manager for SharePoint, we had almost a thousand pieces of press coverage for the product in a single year. Big vendors win coverage and analyst attention. They get word of mouth and media buzz. They lead the discussions about categories and trends.

How Big is Your Market?

Let's return to the issue of market size. The size of your market matters for a number of reasons. For one thing, it can tell you how much of your product you can expect to sell. I was once involved in developing software which could only be used by movie studios and large media distribution companies. This is not a good idea when you have only 20 potential customers in the entire world. You're not going to sell very much software. That market was probably about $20 million a year. Given the number of incumbents, it was impossible to carve out any meaningful revenue for ourselves.

The discussion of market size for enterprise technology products brings to mind a hilarious comment made at an SOA conference a number of years ago. The speaker said something to the effect of, "SOA is now encountering an unforeseen obstacle on its way to becoming the de-facto enterprise architectural standard: reality." Official prognostications are great, but they are not usually very helpful for gauging how much of your product you can actually sell. Industry firms may estimate your market at some (typically very high) level but this number may be totally meaningless in actual sales and marketing terms.

How do research firms come up with market sizes which are not realistic? One problem stems from research firms' tendency to correlate relatively open-ended questions with hard numerical estimates. A research survey might ask IT managers their budget for a certain category of technology. The categories offered as choices may be vague or aspirational, e.g. "Unified Communications and Collaboration" (UCC). One survey taker might consider UCC to include all productivity software, such as groupware and Intranet software, while another might think UCC refers only to VOIP hardware. The first person says he will spend $10 million on UCC in the next year, while the other says he will spend $50,000. Both are right, and the result can be a hugely inflated market size estimate.

A better way to estimate the true size of your market is to add up the sales volumes of your closest competitors in the relevant categories. This information may be hard to find, though you can develop ways of estimating the figures. Let's say you sell a certain type of hardware appliance. You know that you sell $5 million a year worth of this product and you have several direct competitors of similar size. You think that each of them sells between $3 and $10 million each. A very large technology company also sells a similar product. However, even though is a multi-billion dollar company, you estimate, based on articles you have read and other commentary available online, that they sell $40 million a year of their product. Your market size and share breakdown looks like this:

Table 9 – Sizing the industry by reviewing closest and largest competitors.

	Sales	Share
You	$ 5,000	7%
Competitor 1	$ 3,000	4%
Competitor 2	$ 7,000	10%
Competitor 3	$ 4,500	6%
Competitor 4	$ 10,000	14%
Large Vendor	$ 40,000	58%
Total Market	$ 69,500	100%

In the assessment shown in Table 9, your company has a 7% share of a market, which is about $70 million. Is this good or bad? It's hard to say. However, if the industry research firms peg your market at $1 billion, you will be seen as having one half of one percent of the market. Ouch! That is so small that you might be completely dismissed by buyers and analysts. If the market is perceived as tiny, investors will not be happy. Do you want your investors to think you're in a small market? Yet, if the market is small you can look as if you have a bigger share of it. How many metaphors can I mix in describing this terrible dilemma? It is a double-edged sword, a fool's errand full of narrow risky straits, rocks and hard places, and Catch 22s.

Market Dynamics vs. Market Size

To give you some consolation, I am pretty sure the biggest successes in the tech industry were also muddled about the size and definition of their respective markets from time to time. In most cases, the true breakouts establish what the market is, and everyone else follows. So, just be a big success and none of this will matter. How hard could it be?

Seriously, the best approach to understanding your market is to focus on what customers are going to buy from you in the next year or two. This is a process which does not necessarily have to align with your analyst briefings and official boilerplate. What are people buying today? What is similar to your product, and who is selling it? Who is buying it? Here is your market.

SoftCo is thinking about selling a portal and image file management system. Like it or not, they have to face the fact that they have some very big competitors in their market. They're going to be going up against Microsoft SharePoint, IBM FileNet and WebSphere Portal, EMC Documentum and OpenText.

In a market analysis we are not going to delve into specific product-to-product comparisons. We need to understand the market dynamics. And, as the table below shows, segments really matter when you're trying to figure out market dynamics. The tensions and opportunities are quite different depending on whom you are talking to about a particular technology purchasing choice. The case shown in Table 10 is meant be illustrative, not necessarily reflecting a specific reality or definitive point of view of the market.

Table 10 – Segmenting a market by size and exploring relevant market dynamics in each segment.

Segment	Dominant Players	Market dynamics	Possible strategies
Large Enterprise	• IBM • EMC	Large-scale, long-lived vendor deals predominate, with resulting content management "religion." Large system integrators (including IBM Global Technology Services) implement the systems.	Create a compatible plug-in or system extension to enable SoftCo functionality exposed to end user. Affiliate with large system integrators.
Medium Enterprise	• Microsoft • OpenText	In-house developers buy content management solutions that are customized to work with Microsoft SharePoint or OpenText. In some cases, they work with Microsoft system integrator partners.	Integrate with Microsoft and OpenText products. Cultivate reseller relationships with SI partners.

One thing you have to figure out right away is which segments will buy your product at all? If your product is not enterprise grade, then you will not sell it into large companies no matter how good your relationships are with big system integrators. Similarly, if your product is priced for large enterprises and has features which make it costly to administer, it will not sell in to medium-size businesses, generally speaking. In practical terms, a given market segment might have a value of zero for your specific situation.

If your product can be sold in either segment, you need to figure out your probability of success factoring in the dynamics of the segments. Your realistic overall market sizing based on realistic dynamics might look like the following one shown in Table 11:

Table 11 – Market sizing based on potential deals available.

	Number of Potential Customers	% Currently in Market for Product	Number of Potential Deals per Year	Average Deal Size	Total Annual Revenue
Large Enterprise	2,500	10%	250	$ 100,000	$ 25,000,000
Medium-Sized Enterprises	12,000	10%	1200	$ 20,000	$ 24,000,000
Total Market					$ 49,000,000

There are a couple of big assumptions built into this model. The percent of customers currently "in market" for the product is a serious one. Of course, every large enterprise in the world could buy your product, which in this case would represent a gross market size of $250 million. Wow! Yet we all know there are incumbents and customers which are not going to change their existing product or add a new capability in any given year. As a result, we can determine a more realistic segmented market.

Then, we have to figure out how much we can actually sell given the market dynamics. Knowing the product requires some type of system integrator partner, we need a realistic assessment of how many deals we can do. In Table 12 below, we estimate how many SI partners our company can realistically find, sign, and support. Then we estimate how many deals each partner can bring in and fulfill in a given year. This brings us to segment totals. Note that the medium-sized enterprise segment looks more appealing based on the number of partners and deals which it can support. Perhaps we will want to focus only on this segment.

Table 12 - Estimating projected revenue based on partners and deal flow.

	Number of SI Partners Who Can be Engaged	Deals Per Year Per SI	Total Deals	Total Projected Revenue
Large Enterprise	5	8	40	$ 4,000,000
Medium sized enterprises	30	15	450	$ 9,000,000
Total projected revenue	35		490	$ 13,000,000

This estimation process gives us two other things to think about. One is market share. A realistic market share goal for this company would be 27%, or $13 million in revenue in a 49% market. This is a much more useful number than 1% of a billion dollar market, or some such figure you might get from working the industry reports. Also, a huge factor to consider in this type of thought process is how many deals can your organization realistically support? This is often a surprise for people who are coming into enterprise technology for the first time. Honestly, there is an upper limit to how many customer engagements a tech firm can support. You have to go through an honest appraisal of what your company's attainable market share goals can be, given those constraints.

A small digression is in order. If you sell enterprise technology you will be involved in customer support. The more complex and expensive your solution, the more intense the support demands will be. This limits your ability to scale revenue. Ideally, over time your product will become easier to support and require less. In the near term however, it is almost always the case that support issues limit growth for enterprise technology companies.

Dominance is the other big market dynamics factor which influences market sizing exercises. If one vendor dominates a category or customer segment, this will affect your ability to penetrate that market. Your estimate of attainable market share should reflect realities of dominance. In some cases, dominance is so complete as to make the whole discussion irrelevant. How big is the market for "Information Worker Productivity Tools"? Well, there is a big market. It's in the neighborhood of $20 billion! Should you care? I think not. Microsoft has well over 90% of this market. The industry is littered with the wreckage of companies which have tried to take market share away from Microsoft Office. The remaining percentage is filled with open-source solutions and specialized tools. So, we have a $20 billion market sandbox, which you won't be playing in unless you decide to partner with Microsoft. Then, you're in a different discussion altogether.

If SoftCo wanted to hop on board the Microsoft Office wagon, it could create some hooks into Office, which would enable Office users to gain access to the SoftCo photo portal. They could create a tool bar button for PowerPoint, which would show PowerPoint users photos that were available in SoftCo for placement in a slide deck. There are a lot of PowerPoint users out there (Office has about 500,000,000 users worldwide, though not all are on the 2007 or 2010 editions which have the toolbar.) In this way, it is possible leverage a market which is essentially closed.

Not that it will be closed forever. Even Microsoft Office is starting to feel encroachment from various mobile and non-Microsoft alternatives. Tablets and smart phone devices appear to be chipping away at Microsoft's dominant position. So, while I wouldn't advise anyone trying to build a business today to take on Office, it is illustrative to try to see who is pulling ahead. If one vendor is pulling out of the herd and moving ahead quickly, this is an important sign to watch for in understanding the dynamics of the market.

The "pulling ahead" phenomenon counts for a number of reasons. On a practical level, if one product is gaining momentum in the market, it may sway potential customers to go with this product. It becomes a self-fulfilling prophecy, where the one pulling ahead takes over the market. On the level of optics, it looks good for the product which pulls ahead. It seems they are doing something right lending credibility to their fund-raising efforts, whether from VCs or internal budgets.

Just to confound you a bit, consider the effects of market mass in contrast to speed. In some cases, a single vendor will pull ahead and quickly start to dominate a category, only to be rolled back by bigger competitors later on. The classic case of this was with BEA and IBM WebSphere. BEA was an early innovator in the Java-based application server market and quickly rose to prominence. Over a period of years, IBM WebSphere relentlessly pushed its way into the category and is today the world's number one app server. BEA was later acquired by Oracle.

Then we have rigidity. Some technologies stick, and stick hard. Mainframes are a great case of this. They are a continuing presence in numerous enterprises despite being eulogized as a dead technology for two decades. It is true that many organizations have replaced mainframes with distributed systems, but a lot of big transactional computing is still done by mainframes, and will continue to be done this way for a long time to come. When you're assessing the dynamics of your market, you need to understand whether you have a rigid component affecting growth prospects for new entrants. If you are in a market segment dominated by rigidity, you usually have more options than just walking away. In the case of the mainframe, there are many companies which have succeeded, by developing middleware which augments mainframe functionality – capitalizing on the rigidity of the mainframe and making it work for their businesses.

If you found this chapter a little confusing, that's probably good. Market definitions should be challenging. If you're excessively confident that you understand exactly what's going on in your industry, you either haven't done enough research or you're in a really boring, mature industry with low valuation growth prospects. It's okay. Ambiguity can be your friend if you know how to work it.

Chapter 6: Understand the Customer

U nderstand the customer. Understand the market. Create preference. Aren't these all basically the same activity? Yes and no. As a technology marketer, one of your most basic jobs is to understand what the customers wants and what he or she will actually buy. The two are not necessarily the same thing. What you can interest people in, and what you can sell them, are often completely different products. This dichotomy is frustrating and perplexing, yet it is a fixture of B2B technology marketing.

The split between customer interest and an actual sale is yet another great difference between B2B technology marketing and consumer marketing. In most marketing scenarios, if you have the attention of the customer, offering them something they want and need at a price they can afford, you are almost all the way to making a sale. Not so with technology marketing. Take the iPad. Though the state of affairs is changing, it has been difficult to sell iPads to corporate buyers to date. Most business people see the iPad and love it. They want it. Indeed, many of them buy it for themselves for personal use in their jobs. However, if you went to the IT department at their companies, you would more likely than not hear something like, "We like the iPad too but we don't support it right now." Period. End of story. You are not going to sell iPads to that customer no matter how much better it may be than comparable tablets.

The iPad situation shows the gulf between the user and the buyer in a B2B technology sale. The people who make the purchase decision are not always the same people who actually use the product. In a lot of cases, the end users want something the company will not buy for them. How could this be, you might wonder? Wouldn't it make sense to equip your workers with the technology they prefer - tools which will help them do a good job? This is complicated. Generally, the IT department is the main purchase decision-maker in a B2B technology sale. And, IT will only buy what it can support. IT cannot acquire every technology the employees want. IT usually commits to service and support technology to some defined level (a "service level agreement" or "SLA") that binds IT to performance criteria. Untested, little understood technologies simply cannot meet these criteria, at least initially.

The problem with many consumer technologies that people want to bring to work is that they lack enterprise management features. For instance, even if Windows isn't your cup of tea, your IT department benefits from all types of elaborate management systems which help it oversee thousands of Windows PCs without spending too much money and tying up a myriad of personnel. Not all personal computing technologies come with this option of administrative support technology.

Even proven enterprise technologies cannot always be adopted if they cannot muster support. You might love an Oracle application, but if your company is an "IBM shop," it may be a tough sell. There are good reasons for this, in business terms. When an IT department commits to a given technology it creates an efficiency which is hard to replicate when there are too many varieties of technology to maintain.

Does this mean the end user opinions are unimportant in B2B technology marketing? Not at all. End users are extremely important in the equation, though they almost always lack actual purchasing authority. Business managers are not stupid. They want their people to have the right tools to do their work and they will usually listen when people suggest or request new technologies in the workplace. In cases where a business does acquire a new technology, very often an end user, or users, will be recruited to serve as a "champion" of the product to ensure broad adoption. Today, we even have the "Bring Your Own Device" (BYOD) trend where corporate IT is expected to support whatever phone or tablet people want to use at work. Searching for the champion can and should occur before the sales process is finished. Smart technology vendors identify potential champions early on in the sales and marketing cycle, hoping to build enthusiasm for a new technology in the workplace which will translate into management support and an IT-driven purchase decision.

News Flash: There is No Customer

There is no customer in B2B technology marketing. What? That's right - there really is no customer. There is only a committee of people who evaluate and purchase products. If you need to think of a "customer," imagine a hydra-headed creature combining all the elements shown in the Tables 13 through 15 below. I like to think of the customer as a group of personas in a hierarchy of engagement with the product purchase process. Each level of the hierarchy is important to the process, but each plays a different role.

Table 13 – Defining key customer personnel in the purchase decision.

	Role in Purchase Process	Optimal Marketing Approach
End User	Though not always considered, their point of view can weigh very heavily on decision makers.	Market to the end user emphasizing features that will make their lives easier
Influencer	People whose opinions matter in the purchase process.	Understand their pain and speak to it.
Decision Maker	The person who can pull the trigger.	Understand their pain, in the context of their relationships with end users and influencers... and speak to it.

Your customer is a composite of multiple points of view held by the group of people who influence the purchase decision. Table 14 attempts to organize the composite by plotting each individual's functional role and his or her purchase influence on two axes. Big as it is, the chart is nonetheless a simplistic representation of the personas involved in an enterprise technology sale. On the X axis, we have the three levels of influence. On the Y axis, we list the stakeholder roles. Roughly, these roles break into business and IT.

Stakeholder roles include basics such as "Individual User" and "Line of Business (LOB) Manager" but also "Group." Who is "Group?" There is not anyone named "group" at most companies. What I want you to understand is that the group of people that uses the product is itself a stakeholder, even if there is no specific individual you can speak to about the group's needs and wants. Good LOB managers will consider the overall group's perspective on a technology before they recommend purchasing it.

Table 14 – Expanded customer role chart showing purchase influences.

	Defined as	End User	Influencer	Decision Maker
Business Level				
Individual User	Information Worker	X		
Group	Marketing Dept.	X		
LOB Manager	Marketing Director		X	
LOB Executive	VP of Marketing			X
IT level				
Operations	Support Desk Personnel		X	
Developer				
Security			X	
Architect			X	
IT Manager	Director of IT for Marketing		X	

Imagine SoftCo wants to understand who the "customer" is when it sells its photo portal to a marketing department. Understanding the customer(s) in this situation will drive sales and sales support work streams (e.g. collaterals, how to craft the proposal, how to demo the software, etc.) By filling out the chart shown above, they can assign end user/influencer/decision-maker status to each of the buyer personas with whom they are dealing in the sales process. Here is how it plays out: This is not an IT critical sale such as a firewall or server, so IT in this case is an influencer, but not a decision-maker. IT will have to endorse the final selection, and they must be treated with great care. However, the purchase order will be signed by the VP of Marketing. It will come out of her budget.

The chart will look different depending on the customer situation. The challenge is to see the path to building preference according to the lineup of influencers and decision-makers. You'll need to figure out what each buyer persona needs and communicate that you can and will deliver it. What is their pain? What keeps them up at night? You solve it. The challenge comes in trying to understand and address so many different points of view.

Table 15 – Identifying pain points and solutions for each relevant buyer persona.

	Defined as	Pain	Solution
Individual User	Information Worker	Can't find images easily	Searchable image repository with metadata and tagging
Group	Marketing Dept.	Multiple image repositories to manage and use	Single repository of images
LOB Manager	Marketing Director	Needs more productivity from people on team	Less time looking for images translates into greater productivity
LOB Executive	VP of Marketing	Wants faster execution of projects	More product teams being productive by using the portal
Operations	Support Desk Personnel	Tired of fielding the same question about how to download an image over and over	Browser-based portal hosted on standard server is easier to support
Developer		N/A	
Security		Images are information assets that need to be secured, but most repositories make it hard to do so.	Security settings feature enables security management for asset repository.
Architect		N/A	
IT Manager	Director of IT for Marketing	Adding systems means adding support budget, which is not possible.	This portal enables consolidation of image repositories, resulting in fewer systems to maintain.

The End Goal: Narrowing the Customer Committee

Of all these personas, some will inevitably count more than others. One seldom sees a situation where everyone's voice is equal in driving preference and selection. Who really matters in this configuration? The trick is to target who has the greatest pain and who has the greatest influence over the purchase. This will help. Consider giving each buyer persona a score for his level of pain and influence. If you assigned a number between 1 and 5 for pain and influence, the highest scoring persona would be the one whom you want to target. At the same time, address the needs of the other members of the customer committee. If you can balance your approach and message in this way, you should be able to move the preference needle with the whole group.

Understanding the customer – or collection of influencers, if you will – is a never-ending task. The important thing to bear in mind is, there isn't any single customer. There is always a group. How the group functions and who is in control of it will vary from client to client. It is up to the sales team to figure out the specifics of how to approach any given account. However, as the marketer, your job is to understand the dynamics of the generic group. In the case of a firewall, for instance, you might be able to generalize quite accurately as to the group in charge of making the selection. You know it will be people involved in information security. You can make assumptions (and test them) about how the purchase decision is made, as well as who the champions and influencers will be. With those assumptions in mind, you can develop go-to-market messaging and strategies which will pave the way for sales success.

CHAPTER 7: INFORM

PRODUCT DESIGN

Some technology marketers are involved in product design, but not all. The term used most often in describing marketers who contribute to product design, is "Product Marketing." Sometimes, the phrase "Product Management" refers to this function, though Product Management is more typically a role involving basic marketing on behalf of a specific product.

I mention this because marketing people need to be involved in product design but their input is not always welcome. The title "Product Marketing" suggests a responsibility for Product Design input. In my experience, however, marketing's involvement in product development will be greeted with reactions which range from, "Go jump in a lake" to "Thank you for sharing...we'll get back to you." Sometimes there can be real cooperation. For marketing to have a seat at the product development table, there usually has to be some executive level support for the idea. Otherwise, it is prone to failure.

Your role in product development will also depend on the size of the company and marketing organization. In some cases, there is a specific product marketing function which has a distinct responsibility for researching customer needs and collaborating with engineers on product design. However, most of the time, the connection is a bit more tenuous. But, marketing absolutely should be involved in product development. One reason is that marketing's own success or failure will depend, to a great extent, on the product itself. A lot of fired marketing executives were guilty only of being forced to market a product the market did not want.

Product Marketing Process Overview

First, let's get an overview of how this is supposed to work. There are myriad variations on the pattern, but the cycle shown in Figure 11 summarizes most approaches to product marketing. At the beginning, the product marketer tries to figure out what customers need and what the market will reward – which is not necessarily the same thing, as we sometimes see. This stage is known as *"requirements gathering."* Gathering requirements may involve market research, discussions with clients and prospects, competitor analysis, as well as analysis of deals which were lost. Sometimes this last one is the most important but it is often neglected because the soul-searching involved can be too challenging.

A huge list of basic requirements is helpful, but it won't get you where you want to go in terms of producing a commercially successful product. To guide developers, you will need to merge the raw requirements with your company's strategy and strengths. The result will be a document known as a *"Marketing Requirements Document"* or MRD. MRDs come in a lot of different shapes and sizes, but they generally contain the following sections:

- Market overview

- Customer profile and "buyer persona"

- Key requirements - Have to have

- Secondary requirements - Nice to have

- Product roadmap

- Go-to-market plan, including partner strategy

The MRD is a consensus piece, essentially. It can be long or short – I've seen them range from four pages to fifty. The way this is put together depends on the way your organization blends marketing and product development. The main goal is to use the MRD as marketing's input into the development process. MRD and marketing input follows a cycle, shown in Figure 11. The first step is determining what customers want through some type of research. Then, after the list of basic requirements has been generated, you need to mesh them with relevant facts on the ground, such as company strategy and how the product is engineered. What if your research indicates your clients desperately want Adobe Flash video in a product built to support Windows Media? This is a factor which will need to be addressed in engineering. It is not a deal breaker, but it does complicate matters.

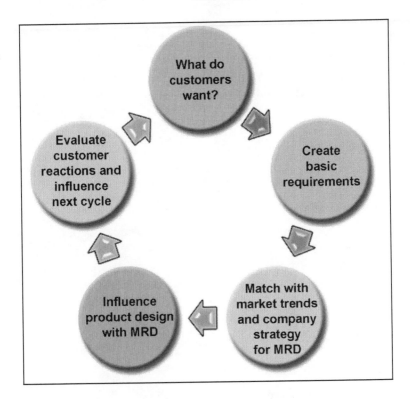

Figure 11 - The product marketing cycle.

As the product development process continues, the MRD can be a touchstone for engineering and Management to come together and agree on which features will be included in upcoming releases of the product. The engineering twin of the MRD is the *"Product Requirements Document"* or PRD. Sometimes it will all be the <u>same</u> document.

Should You Do Market Research?

I have to disclose that my wife is a professional market researcher and focus group moderator, so even asking this question is heresy. In some industries, serious market research is a basic requirement of doing business. In my wife's case of pharmaceutical marketing, research is a fundamental part of the business process. Few major marketing decisions are made in that industry without structured research and deep analysis. But, having worked in technology for a while, I have some insight into which situations demand rigorous market research and which do not.

Tech Market Research Overview

I will digress for a moment into the different forms of market research so we can all be on the same page. We all know what market research is, right? Yet, when we really try to define it, the clarity starts to fall apart. At least, it does for me. As a result, I thought I would start this section of the book with a little overview of market research. If your brain is perfect, unlike mine, you can skip ahead.

Market research, broadly speaking, is any activity you undertake to achieve a better understanding of the market, competitors and customer. There is a spectrum of possible approaches to market research, some of which are better than others for a given objective. Market research is yet another area, however, where the B2B tech industry is different from consumer-facing industries or other more conventional business marketing endeavors. The culprit, as always, is the shape-shifting categories which we find ourselves in. What market are you in? This is such a basic question but one which is hard to answer accurately much of the time if you market technology in the B2B context. If you don't know what market you're in, how can you research it? You may, of course, but some of the traditional approaches to research don't hold up very well.

Original vs. Published

You have two broad choices when it comes to market research. You can buy published research or do your own. Conducting your own may or may not involve engaging a specialized agency. Published research, which includes industry reports and assessments of new technologies may be helpful, but also prone to inaccuracies. The tech industry is constantly in flux and categories are hard to pin down. In this context, you can form wildly wrong conclusions from reading a published report. I have seen so many examples of estimates of industry size or dynamics, which simply don't match reality. As in, if you were looking at the mobile phone industry in 2005, Apple wasn't even on the map. A few years later, **it was the map**.

Doing your own research is generally a better, if more costly approach. You can form your own hypothesis to test and figure out what you want to learn for your specific situation. That said, it is also easy to fall into many different types of thinking traps when you do your own research. We are all victims of our own paradigms, which were formed by our experiences, so you run the risk of designing a research project confirming whatever possibly erroneous view that you already hold.

Formal vs. Informal Market Research

You also have a choice whether you want to do what I call either formal or informal market research. I don't think this is an industry standard term, but the difference between the two approaches should be clear. Formal market research involves collecting data in a systematic way from individuals who are (hopefully) blind to the entity gathering the information. Formal research is almost always performed by a third party agency or contractor with a data collection questionnaire, which they develop with you to achieve your research goals. There two basic types of formal market research:

- **Quantitative** – In quantitative market research, customers are typically asked a narrowly focused range of questions on the research topic, with multiple choice, yes/no, or "ratings" type of questions. The answers can be tabulated as uniform data and presented as statistically relevant findings if the sample size is large enough. For example, when Trident gum says "4 out of 5 dentists who chew gum recommend sugarless gum..." this is a statistically meaningful statement (we hope) based on a market research survey. To get to that finding, Trident had to interview some large number of dentists – a large enough sample to make the claim valid. If they interviewed 5 dentists and got 4 to say they preferred sugarless gum, it wouldn't be valid. Examples of quantitative market research execution include phone surveys, interviews, and online surveys.

- **Qualitative** – Qualitative is all about depth and subjectivity. Qualitative research does not generally yield statistically relevant findings. However, it can offer real insights into customer behavior and preferences if it is executed correctly. Two approaches to qualitative research predominate:

  o Individual Interview – This technique provides good, subjective insight into the customer though with the least statistical relevance. This is only one person's opinion. However, if a researcher talks to 20 individuals and finds many of them hold similar points of view on an issue, this is a directional finding. A more intense variant of the individual interview is known as the in-depth interview (IDI). The can take an hour or more, giving the interview the opportunity to probe and ask follow up questions about ideas that emerge in the discussion. In most cases, customers are paid for their time.

o Group Interview (Focus Group) – This is a better known qualitative research technique wherein a group of customers or prospects are gathered into a discussion room, which usually features a two way mirror so clients and agency personnel can observe the proceedings. In a focus group, a moderator takes the group through a series of open-ended questions, facilitates discussion amongst the members and probes for more information when a discussion is trending in a direction which will deliver insights towards the research objectives. Focus groups can yield valuable insights into how people interact with one another to form opinions on a marketing topic. The group often encourages people to talk more, though unfortunately groups may be hijacked by domineering personalities. For these and other reasons, almost every focus group project requires conducting at least two groups. In most cases, focus group participants are paid for their time.

In both the IDI and focus group examples, the researcher prepares a report on findings from the research. The unanalyzed results, such as transcripts, can be revealing, but as the marketer, you probably want someone to summarize and synthesize the findings.

Informal market research is similar to formal, but it is essentially homemade. Examples of informal research include customer focus groups and user group discussions. It is also relatively simple and inexpensive to put together a survey online and blast it out to your email list. Here is the benefit of what is right about informal market research: It's cheap. Do not underestimate the value of this aspect. It is intimate, and shows your customers you are listening. You are being direct. This is a dialogue between your company and its key stakeholders. It can be a lot faster than formal research. The formal market research process can be lengthy, perhaps by necessity. To clarify objectives and produce an effective interview guide, recruit candidates, interview them, and then process the raw data, you are looking at a minimum of 2-4 months. Informal work can be executed more quickly. This, however, is also one of its major drawbacks.

The immediacy and rapid pace of informal research can be as much of a problem as it is a blessing. Talking with your customers about your products and future plans has several major drawbacks:

- This is not a blind study – People tend to be a lot more honest when they don't know who they are talking to, or about, in a market research study. If you are speaking directly with someone who has already bought your product, you are not going to understand the type of drivers of why they chose you over a competitor. There is a relationship already in existence, which will influence the discussion no matter how hard you try to obscure it. Customers may not want to hurt your feelings, or insult the engineers who made the product. Or, they may be disappointed with the product and express a lot of negativity, which doesn't necessarily reflect the product reality.

- You may be hung up on specific irritants – Client focus groups are notorious for devolving into a game of "You said you would add this feature a year ago. Why have you not done so?" The customer's frustration with whatever the issue may be – customer support, performance, etc. – will trump any productive research discussion.

- You yourself become myopic - The best research opens up the thought process and discovers new findings. In a client focus group, concentrating only on topics which are relevant to the customers and to your development team, you run a huge risk. This may make short term business sense, but you're missing a lot of potential findings by not asking broader, more open-ended questions. Imagine you have a Java application running on a Tomcat server. Your biggest customer is hung up on wanting your app to run on WebSphere. You therefore ask your client focus group how much they want the app to run on WebSphere. What you don't ask them, but which they might tell you if you knew how to probe with open ended questions, is that they actually want the app to run on JBOSS.

- It takes a lot of work – Good market research takes a lot of work. Chances are, you don't have the resources to do it properly yourself on a regular basis. Some companies set up a customer council and have a great first meeting. Then, six months later, at the second meeting, the marketing team is not prepared for the discussion. They might not have the bandwidth to do the intensive work of establishing research objectives or creating a discussion guide. The second meeting falls flat. The third meeting is an embarrassment. The fourth gets postponed. The group never meets again. Your customers think you are flaky and you've learned very little.

Getting Input From Sales

You are going to want to talk to your sales team and get their input on the market, what customers want, and the type of features which should be added to the product. This is absolutely essential. After all, the sales people are right out there in front of the clients, facing off against competitors. They know what sells. But, be careful. Sales can get hung up on what they need to sell something right now, not what the wisest long-term product strategy might be. Sales people can also be very persuasive (this is their job, isn't it?) in convincing you to buy into their view of what the product needs. It will be necessary to filter input from sales to remain focused on what is best for the product for the long haul.

Competitive analysis is another necessary but tricky aspect of doing informal market research. You have to do it. You would be derelict in your duties as a marketing professional if you didn't. Yet, you have to face the limits of competitive research. On one level, unless you are going to buy your competitors' products and tear them apart – something most big companies do – your insights into the competitor offerings will be fairly limited. You can try to convince customers to give you their opinions on your competitors, but many people feel uncomfortable doing so. It will depend on your relationship. The best competitive insights often come, unfortunately, when you lose a sale to a competitor. If you can figure out why you lost, this knowledge will tell you a lot. Otherwise, you are stuck with analyzing the public record, which is not always useful. You will find your competitor's product feature has its claims online, but you won't know how well they work. You may see list pricing, but you won't see how they really charge. Analysts can be helpful, but even these folks can be influenced to think one way or another – and they are often wrong.

The bigger picture about competitive analysis and all of these research techniques is that they tend to trap you in what is already happening. They limit your thinking to products that are currently in favor with the market. Anyone doing market research should reflect on the fact that Steve Jobs, arguably the most successful technology entrepreneur ever, did not believe in market research. As Jobs famously said, it wasn't the customers' job to tell him what they wanted. Sometimes, true free thinking is the best market research.

What Does the Market Really Want?

Not all of us (or any of us) can claim the technology marketing genius of Steve Jobs. We can take a cue from him, though, and try to be circumspect about market research. Research will definitely tell you important things to understand about the customer and the market, assuming you are ready to listen. It can also lead you astray. The best practice is to try to take it all in - formal research, informal research, purchased research - and blend it with your own thoughts and your own gut instinct about what is really going on in the market. If you've been working in a particular sector for a while, you are going to have your own ideas about what is going to work in the market and what isn't. The trick is to trust your intuition but allow yourself to see critical findings in the research process. You may conclude ultimately that you are wrong, but don't sell yourself short.

Partnering with Engineering

Partner with engineering. I know. Sorry. Don't you hate those MBA terms like "partner with engineering"? I do, in general, but in this case, it is actually a good idea. Like it or not, you are going to have to work closely with engineering to get your views on the product heard and implemented. This can be a necessary relationship. Though engineering and marketing are typically on opposite sides of a tech business, it doesn't have to be this way. For the relationship and working partnership to be successful, you need to take the initiative to overcome a few major obstacles.

- **Take the time to understand the product from an engineering perspective** – While you may not ever truly understand the product at the code object level, you need to understand how the product works under the surface. This will help you assess possible changes to the product in terms of difficulty and expense. A lot of product ideas may seem cool, but when you evaluate them in the context of effort required to implement, you may see them differently. For example, it might seem appealing to adapt your product to integrate with a mainframe. However, you have to be sure there really is a market for the integration before you set out on what can be a pretty costly and complex process.

- **Get to know your engineering counterparts** – This sounds simple but it is often overlooked. Engineers are people, too. Get to know them. Having a personal connection will help you both as a listener and as an advocate of marketing's perspective on the product roadmap.

- **Respect that engineering has its own plans and goals** – You may have a sudden inspiration, which seems like a no brainer. "Yes, we need a WebSphere portlet! Can you make it tomorrow?" "Uh…. No." The engineering team is usually hard at work, adhering to a plan that was set out for them before you got involved. Asking them to drop everything may not be a wise call. Going over their heads and getting a high level dictum requiring them to drop everything for your sudden inspiration or self-propelled change in product strategy is not going to make you any friends.

- **Earn your credibility** – A lot of engineers look at marketing as merely the people who make things look pretty. In some cases this is true, but not all tech marketers are superficial. You probably won't rise to the level of the engineering knowledge they have, but you could be a quick study, and show you understand the engineering process. For example, if your engineering team uses an agile software development methodology, you should try to get your head around how this process works. You should have an appreciation for the develop-test-release process. Understand that good engineering takes time and talented people.

The Roadmap

Product management is a process, which ideally blends long and short term planning. There is what is happening right now, but if you're doing your job correctly, you should have your eye on the future. Most product managers create a "product roadmap" to express how everyone believes the product should evolve over the next, say, five years. Figure 12 below is a rough approximation of a roadmap. At each interval, perhaps a year, a major new platform integration is planned.

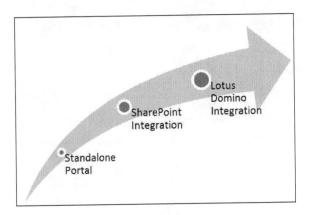

Figure 12 - Simplified product roadmap.

The roadmap exists for several purposes. For one thing, this is about having agreement – or the appearance of agreement – on where the product is going. The roadmap is also a concession to the reality that most teams can only do one major update at a time. It is often wishful thinking at best to imagine that everything planned on the roadmap is going to happen. No one really knows where the market is going to be in five years, or which new technologies will be affecting product management decisions.

Finally, the sales team is a major stakeholder in the roadmap. In most large scale technology sales, there are client requirements which simply cannot be addressed by the current state of the product. No single product can satisfy every demand made by an enterprise. As a result, sales people want to show their clients and prospects a product roadmap which demonstrates a commitment to making the changes in the specific product the client wants.

CHAPTER 8: ADVISE SENIOR LEADERSHIP ON CORPORATE STRATEGY AND ORGANIZATION

Marketing is part of every company's strategic mix. The direction a company decides to take should be based on an understanding of the market and trends which affect their business. As a marketer, you should have a voice in the strategic decision-making process. In the implementation of the strategy, you need to be able to advise senior managers on the structure of the marketing organization itself.

Unless you are a marketing bigshot in a large company, however, you may view the idea of advising senior leadership on strategy and the marketing organization as being a bit above your pay grade. You may have more of a voice than you realize, though. When VPs of marketing and CMOs need to advise their bosses, the CEOs and COOs, they may turn to you for comment. (If they are smart they will.) Plus, if you plan on moving up, you should learn to think about the bigger strategic and organizational picture.

In a small company environment, you should definitely have a point of view on strategy and the marketing organization. In the intimate executive suite of a startup, for example, there can be many direct discussions about strategy and organizational shape amongst senior operational, marketing, engineering, finance, and sales managers. If you speak for marketing, you need to have at least one cent (or maybe two cents) on the topic.

Even defining "strategy" as it relates to marketing can be a bit challenging. Strategy is one of those words that is used, misused, misunderstood and overused. It is a word which can be used to inspire discussions, hurled as a threat, or a catch-all "shut up" switch. Invoking strategy is a great way to purport moving a discussion to a higher level, thus leaving lower level thinkers out of the mix. It is helpful in this context, to think about strategy in terms of two broad constructs: High level corporate strategy, and marketing related strategy.

High level corporate strategy is the domain of Michael Porter and his classic work, *Competitive Strategy*. Strategic discussions in this realm have to do with erecting barriers to entry in a marketplace, creating economies of scale, and protecting earnings growth over the long term. High level strategy has a lot to do with marketing, of course, but this is not really about marketing. Deciding to acquire a firm with a patent portfolio, as a case in point, is not a marketing decision. Where you may be pulled into the discussion, however, is on the significant front of "can we actually make this work?"

Marketing becomes involved in strategy when the discussion moves to competition, alliances and partnerships. While some technology products are successful on a stand-alone basis, most require an alliance of some sort to move you into the market. What if your product were an add-on made specifically for Microsoft Exchange Server? In this case, your alliance strategy is extremely clear: You are part of the Microsoft ecosystem. The Microsoft channel is potentially your channel. Their release cycle affects your release cycle, and so on. A broader example might be a decision to make your product compatible with the Linux operating system. In this case, you are allying yourself with the Linux community, and perhaps some Linux vendors, such as RedHat. This is partly a matter of technology strategy, of course. However, the way your company builds products to fit within alliances and channel partnerships is also very much a marketing matter.

Understanding strategy involves seeing where your product fits into an ever-shifting ecosystem of technologies, products, vendors, partners, and trends. Where are you today? Where do you want to be in a year? This discussion does not occur in a vacuum. Your competitors are constantly innovating and devising new ways of expanding their market share – effectively putting you out of business. How will you react?

Though they are surely gag-inducing, I am going to use the terms "holistic" and "high level" to describe how you can best assess your strategic options. Gag, because these terms are overused. Yet, hate them as you might, they are indeed the most apt way to get at effective strategic thinking. The subtext of this thought is that strategic discussions about competitors, alliances and partners are prone to devolving into engineering vs. sales-driven chest-beating about which features the company needs in order to win deals *now*. Similarly, strategic discussions of partnership can go into rat holes about which partner is the easiest to sign or the partner most aggressively courting you. As a marketer, you are in a position to offer a more holistic and high level view of what is going on and how the company needs to plot its course.

You also have to be customer-centric. Figure 13 below summarizes how I would approach a strategy discussion. The customer is at the center. But, you need to include future customers along with existing ones. From there, every discussion about the product, channel, or alliance strategy, as well as competition, should relate back to how these present and future customers will react.

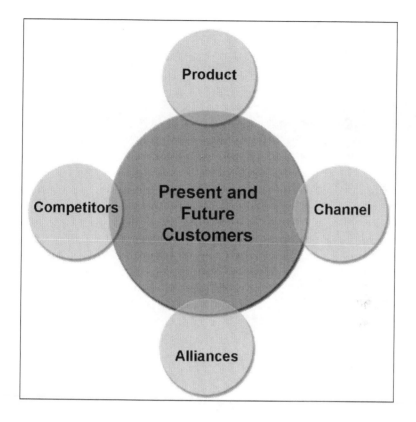

Figure 13 – The holistic view of the customer, keeping in mind product, competition, channel, and alliances.

Imagine you're sitting at the executive staff meeting reviewing SoftCo's strategic options. Each option will have an impact on customers, alliances, channel, and product. There are three options on the table, each of which has specific ramifications for SoftCo's market. Table 16 below summarizes how you can think about these interdependent issues. This example of course goes with my standard disclaimer that this is a completely hypothetical and should not be taken as a true reflection of any particular technology in the real world.

Let's assume the following current situation: SoftCo is a Java-based application which is currently supported on the Apache application server running on Linux.

Table 16 – Strategic options, viewed through multiple lenses of competition, customer impact, effect on alliances, etc.

Strategic Option	Definition	Impact on Present and Future Customers	Competitive Impact	Alliance Impact	Channel Impact	Product/ Operational Impact
Integrate with SharePoint	Surface the SoftCo functionality as a SharePoint Web Part	No impact on present customers. Will be attractive to customers that are standardizing on SharePoint for their intranet portals.	Brings us into competition with various SharePoint-based content management systems, as well as SharePoint itself. However, SharePoint integration makes us appealing to Microsoft shops, compared to incompatible competitors.	The SharePoint technology partner ecosystem is large, but we are not connected to it at all right now. To get included in solutions being developed for SharePoint, we will have to invest in making ourselves a known quantity in this area. We face an obstacle as a non-Microsoft technology – this will have to be overcome through messaging and case studies.	Similarly, there is a huge channel for SharePoint, but we are new to it and will have to work hard on building relationships.	Product is not currently designed for SharePoint compatibility. We will have to invest in development and continued support of this alternative technology.
Be "platform agnostic"	Support any application server or database, including Windows Server, though not integrating with SharePoint per se.	Very appealing for new clients who are on different app servers.	Being able to say "Yes" to virtually any server scenario puts us in a strong position competitively.	We fit into a number of alliance groupings with this approach, including the J2EE community, the WebSphere community, the Solaris and Linux communities, etc. From the database perspective, we fit into the oracle, MySQL and MS SQL alliance groupings.	We can work closely with IBM WebSphere, though we need to be a proven reseller of their server licenses to get much support from them.	Being platform agnostic can mean having serious support challenges, with each customer potentially having a different support scenario – e.g., Solaris 10 and Oracle 11 vs. WebSphere 6.5 and DB2.

As you can see, strategic choices can be messy. There are few easy answers despite the insistence from some that this or that move is a "no brainer." In my experience, the phrase "no brainer" usually indicates a lack of brains in the head of the speaker, who has not delved into the issue enough to understand the complexities involved. However, someone, at some point needs to make a strategic decision.

Your job as a marketer is to understand the marketing implications of a strategic choice and influence the decision-making process accordingly. In this example, you may perceive that being "platform agnostic" is indeed a tremendously powerful marketing option. You can tap into multiple alliances and team up with numerous channel partners. Go for it! Encourage the executive team to go with the platform agnostic approach.

Done, right? Not necessarily. You still have a responsibility to point out a few things. The SharePoint strategy might still be a good idea, and it doesn't necessarily conflict with the platform-agnostic approach. SharePoint is a platform. You can support it along with all other varieties of servers and databases. The Microsoft shops won't care if you also support Java, though Microsoft might not be too keen on helping a company which also aids its rivals. (If you're helping them sell a lot of SharePoint licenses, though, they might not mind so much.)

Okay, are you done now? No, you still have a couple of big "gotchas" to inject into the discussion. If you go for the platform agnostic strategy and perhaps the SharePoint integration strategy as well, you face two potential marketing challenges: You may have service breakdowns as you struggle to support so many different technologies. If the customer experience suffers, this will negatively affect your brand image– a problem which may be hard to correct once it is established as a public fact. On another front, you will almost surely have a slower pace of innovation and release with such a broad strategy than you would have had with a more focused approach to software development. If you are obligated to test every new release on multiple stacks, with myriad database, app server and operating system combinations, not only will you be slow, you will invariably miss some bugs and release defective code. This is just a reality of the business. Again, your image could suffer. Faster rivals could capitalize on these weaknesses and overtake you.

Differentiating Between Partnerships, Alliances, and Channel Relationships

I'm going off the marketing reservation a little bit here and discussing how I personally view the differences between partnerships, alliances, and channel relationships. This discussion may not reflect the mainstream views of the profession, but the truth is there is not much agreement on what these terms mean. Any business relationship between two companies in the technology industry could accurately be referred to as a "partnership," but this generality does us no favors when we try to figure out what is really going to help our strategy. While there is indeed overlap between the concepts of a partner and a channel partner, for example, they are distinctly different relationships. So, feel free to take the following with a grain of salt.

Partnerships

In the technology industry, a partnership occurs when two or more businesses join forces to market their products to a common set of customers. There are myriad possible combinations, but the three most common are the System Integrator (SI), Independent Software Vendor (ISV) and Original Equipment Manufacturer (OEM) approaches.

- **System Integrator** – An SI is in the business of building complete information systems for its clients. Like a contractor building a building, the SI will incorporate a variety of technology products into the system it is creating. From a strategic perspective, SI partners may be a helpful way of extending your reach across a far broader market than you might likely access on your own. This is the case for several reasons. For one thing, the SI usually has long-term, trust-based relationships with clients you probably haven't met. The client prefers to buy from the SI. The SI also usually implements technology in addition to selling it. In most cases, the client wants to purchase a complete solution, and will rely on the SI to deliver it. However, like all potentially great strategic options, SI partners have their good and bad qualities. Ideally, the SI will walk your product into endless new accounts.

However, most SIs need a fair amount of training and prodding to do this The good and big SIs are also often overloaded with vendors trying to get them to build their products into solutions. It is easy for your product to become lost in their noisy environment. Then, if the SI has problems with your technology or needs excessive support, your own resources may quickly be stretched thin.

- **ISV** – And Independent Software Vendor has typically created an application, which runs on one or more operating systems. For example, Intuit is an ISV that makes Quickbooks. Quickbooks runs on Windows. In many cases, ISVs have deep relationships with the large tech companies. For example, there are ISVs specializing in creating financial applications, which run on WebSphere. These ISVs help IBM sell WebSphere licenses.

- **OEM** – An Original Equipment Manufacturer (OEM) is, as its name suggests, a concept borrowed from manufacturing industries. An OEM is a company which supplies parts directly built into a product sold by someone else. Think Bendix Springs. Bendix made the springs, but Ford, GM, and others sold the cars which carried them. Bendix was an OEM for Ford and GM. PCs are full of OEM parts. The outside case may say Dell but the innards come from Panasonic, Intel, and many others. In software, it's the same paradigm, though things may be a bit more abstract. Many software solutions contain elements from other software developers. For example, you might sell an accounting system which ships with Windows Server and Microsoft SQL Server. In this case, Microsoft is an OEM for your product. Software OEMs are common in middleware scenarios. For instance, some platforms come with OEM-created adapters, which connect them to mainframes. Finding a good OEM relationship can be a great boon to your sales efforts. If you are leveraging the sales volume of a big partner, their business will pull yours along. OEM business comes with its own pain, of course. Your margins will likely be lower than if you were selling direct. Support and maintenance issues can also be a challenge.

Alliances

I define an alliance as an agreement between companies or comparable entities to use one another's technologies symbiotically. This may not match everyone's definition of an alliance, but I hope my approach to the concept will provide a useful framework for thinking about the issues involved. In most cases, an alliance is between a small company and a much larger one, or with a large and influential community/organization. For example, a software developer could be allied with Microsoft in both formal and informal terms. The company might be a Gold Partner of the Microsoft Partner Program, formalizing the relationship in the alliance. Informally, and perhaps even more important, the software developer is a "Microsoft shop" and deals with clients who also tend to be "Microsoft shops." Similarly, there are alliances in broader community categories, for instance, such as those surrounding the Linux operating system and Java.

From a strategic perspective, alliances can be defining and essential in both positive and negative directions. Alliances tend to be exclusive, mostly due to the technological challenges of mastering one specific stack. Rarely, some tech companies are platform agnostic. Generally, you're in one alliance or another, even if you don't plan to be. The good part of an alliance is it opens your business to numerous opportunities to sell within the alliance. A J2EE application server "shop" will be a potential client if your product runs on a J2EE server. Alliances provide opportunities for mergers and acquisition (M&A), recruiting, and networking opportunities. Yet, alliances may limit your potential. One example of this, which I bring up at the risk of bodily injury, is the IBM Lotus Domino ecosystem. With absolutely no intention of offending anyone who loves Domino (and people love it, for sure), it is a fairly limited software universe. Certain companies are committed to it. Others have embraced other technologies and will likely never consider Domino-based products in the future.

Channel

Channel relationships involve selling your products through another company. Or, it involves selling someone else's product through your company. This concept should not be alien to you. Car dealers, supermarkets, and gas stations are all examples of channel relationships. In the tech industry, we just give the concept of dealership a fancy name like "channel partner." There are two basic types of channel partners:

- A Value Added Reseller, or VAR – Sells your products as part of a solution that they are building for someone. The concept of a VAR overlaps with that of System Integrators. An SI which resells other products at a markup usually operates as a VAR as well.

- A Value Added Distributor, or VAD – Sells your product as part of a large catalogue. They generally don't build systems. They just sell products. A VAD typically sells many products and serves as an important sales channel for major licensing deals. Companies such as Microsoft and Oracle sell much of their product through VADs, even in cases where the end customer is buying millions of dollars with of software. The VAD processes the order, manages the "paper" of the cash transaction, and connects with the software vendor for management of license IDs.

Partnerships, Strategy and Marketing

Many partnerships in the technology industry blend the SI/VAR/OEM/ISV definitions. Some companies play only one role, but most of the time the SIs are reselling technology from others and profiting from it. VARs do SI work. It all runs together. From a strategy perspective, the main takeaway is that a technology company almost never succeeds all by itself. It is inevitable that your company is going to need to find partners. Or, you may have to assess how your current partnerships are doing and make changes. And of course, you always have to be strategizing about how to best take advantage of your partner relationships to move your business objectives forward. This is where marketing gets involved in the execution of strategy.

Chapter 9: Marketing in a Sales Support Role

There is a popular Website and service called "Marketing Sherpa," which offers specialized research for marketers. The name of the site, however, might describe how a lot of sales people view marketing in general. Oh, marketing? They're our Sherpas. We're climbing the Mt. Everest of sales – the real, hard work in this company – and marketing helps carry our luggage. Good for them! In every company, there is always a question of how marketing and sales should work with one another. Sometimes the relationship is clear, where marketing is the "Sherpa" for sales, assisting and facilitating but not leading. Other times, the process is more about marketing setting the vision and helping sales realize it. It can be balanced, too. In any event, there are certain obligations that marketing always has to sales.

Give Them a Brand to Work With

The best way to think about brand as a sales support issue is to envision how you will deliver visual and verbal consistency to lend the company credibility and identity. A good brand for a business-facing technology company is one which connotes professionalism, quality, and reliability. Opinions will differ on this point, but I have my reasons for believing this. As with so many other aspects of tech marketing, one absolutely must keep the customer clearly in view. For most technology products, the buyer is usually more conservative than your company management. I'm not talking red state-blue state here. I mean, technology buyers are typically risk averse and under pressure to deliver high levels of system availability. Your brand needs to communicate values which support these ideas.

When I was Social Software Evangelist at IBM, I was involved in product management and marketing for Lotus Connections social software for business. Lotus Connections presented an unusual branding challenge for IBM. Social software for business was something new, a cheeky spin on corporate software that borrowed from consumer sites such as Facebook while striving for business legitimacy. The branding, which included the product interface itself, as well as the Website and collaterals, was a great deal-warmer and more Web 2.0-looking than your average IBM business solution. This was intentional. Lotus Connections was trying to look the part. However, the branding was still very much identifiable as IBM, with all the gold-plated seriousness and honor that the brand connotes. Some competitors, though, were not quite getting the idea.

Forgive my exaggeration, but it seemed as though every company which was trying to enter the corporate social software space had a name like "MonkeyPoo" or "Crazanga." These off-the-wall cruh-aaazy entrepreneurs who launched these brands were trying to show how hip and cutting edge they were. They thought this would impress corporate buyers. Wrong. The venture capitalists may have been infatuated with the latest and hippest, but purchasing consideration is not helped by wackiness.

Branding Basics

You owe your sales colleagues (and everyone else involved in the business) some branding basics, including:

- **Name** – It may be too late for you to influence the name of the company, but you can definitely participate in the discussion of new product names. There are many different schools of thought on product naming, but from a branding perspective, you'll find it helpful to have a product naming convention or system. If one product is named after a Native American deity, then the others should be too. It would work against your branding to have three products named "Akna," "Aleut" and "SoftCo Image Manager."

- **Message(s)** – Your message and brand are not necessarily the same thing, but they have to relate and be in alignment with one another. Think about the alignment between your brand, your high-level corporate message, and product-specific messages. Do you they fit together? They should, at least in terms of underlying value proposition. For example, if your corporate message is aspirational and creative, you will have a dissonant brand effect if your product-specific messaging tells the opposite story. For example, if you're "Crazanga: We empower the collaborative mind" but your product message is, "Enterprise Collaboration Suite: Cost effective information worker team site deployment", you're going to have people scratching their heads.

- **Logo, style guide and "brand system"** – You need a distinctive look with the consistent use of fonts, colors, and your logo. This is branding 101. Why do I bother mentioning it? Here is the problem I have seen (and perpetrated, to be honest) at a number of technology companies: most tech companies are founded with engineers who have little interest in marketing and even less money. Typically, they commission a logo and proceed to ignore basic branding style conventions for the next couple of years. This is totally normal and forgivable. After all, when you're trying to build the product, the marketing is an afterthought. Then, when the time has come to go to market, you've got a messy brand on your hands. It is your responsibility to put a strong branding style guide into effect. This includes what is often called a "brand system," which dictates how certain elements work together. For example, if your company has a signature theme, such as a blue swoosh, this swoosh should appear on your PowerPoint decks, Word documents, datasheets, Website, and business cards. This is your distinctive brand element.

Collateral for the Sales Force to Use

You need to keep your sales team supplied with up-to-date datasheets on all of your products. In the modern era, this means PDF documents. Beyond datasheets, you want to paper every offering your company has with supporting documents, which help make the case that your product is the one which deserves preference. Possible ways to accomplish this goal vary from company to company, but I have had success with three basic document types:

- **Technical notes or "Solution Briefs"** – These are short documents, which go into greater depth than the datasheet, and can also cover topics related to the main product details contained in the datasheet. SoftCo might have one datasheet for its basic photo portal. Supporting technical notes could delve into how the product works, the underlying systems which it uses, how it connects with other applications and how it serves specific industry verticals.

- **Technical white papers** – A technical white paper goes into real depth on how a product or solution works. It is intended to satisfy the curiosity and address potential objections of serious technical members of the buying committee.

- **Case studies** – Buyers like to see that people in similar occupations have had a successful experience with your product or solution. A case study needs to demonstrate that your product solved a distinct business problem. Increasingly, case studies are being presented in both written and video form.

Sales Decks

As the marketing person, part of your job is to create sales presentations in PowerPoint (or equivalent non-Microsoft digital files, for my IBM friends out there.) Using your branded PowerPoint template, you need to collaborate with sales to devise an effective presentation, which matches your overall messaging and value proposition. Some marketing people do not consider this to be their responsibility, and they are half right. Yes, sales people are always going to adapt and customize the decks you prepare for them. This is good and bad. The good comes from constant changes in the sales pitch, and the presentation will vary from prospect to prospect. The bad, is that sales people will, with the best of intentions, come up with new marketing concepts on the fly. In my experience, this is not a good situation. You will already have enough trouble wrangling all your marketing content without sales people acting as unmanaged freelancers.

Battle Cards

A battle card is a succinct sales tool usually consisting of a two-sided sheet of paper, meant to help a sales person be a quick study. The card condenses exactly what it takes to sell a particular product or solution. Battle cards vary in content, but most of them contain the following information in brief, digested form:

- The "elevator pitch"

- Key value points of the offering

- Key product facts, i.e. what's new about it, cool features, etc.

- Major objections and how to handle them

- Frequently asked questions

- Competitive differentiation

- Further resource links

Basically, a battle card should have everything a sales person needs to conduct a five minute sales call and get from low awareness to consideration in a potential deal. Marketing is responsible for creating the battle cards. However, making a great battle card involves a skill, which some marketers need to improve, namely listening.

The sales people are really the authors of the battle cards. They are the ones out in the field talking to clients and prospects every day. They have the firsthand knowledge, which will go into the battle card. If you don't listen to what sales has to say, you will create a sub-standard battle card. Your role, though, is to listen and interpret what you hear about discussions in the field and then translate them into hard-hitting, brief attack points, which will push the deal into the pipeline. Of course, you need to align the battle card with other elements of your branding and go-to-market programs.

Proposal Templates

The sales process for enterprise technology invariably involves the development and submission of a written proposal. This can be as simple as a price quote or as elaborate as a massive, multi-media document. I have personally been involved in crafting proposals which are longer than this book. Yikes! Very often, the culprit is a "Request for Proposal" or RFP. These are also known as request for information (RFI) or request for quote (RFQ). No matter what they are called, however, the RFP is a list of questions posed by the customer which the vendor must answer in written form.

Like so many tasks in sales and marketing, different people have different ideas about the right way to do a proposal. Some suggest a very short form with minimal text accompanying the RFP answers. Others even go to the extreme of simply returning the RFP questionnaires (typically in Excel format) with absolutely no explanatory text. In this case, though, I must insist you listen only to me. Seriously, I have worked on proposals now for fifteen years and I have a very good track record of success. I have written proposals which have resulted in millions of dollars of revenue from Fortune 1000 clients. My recommendation is that you develop a proposal template which the sales team can re-use and adapt for multiple sales engagements. The template will be a Word document (or something like it) which the sales person can easily customize for each RFP response.

The best proposals are neither long nor short. They have the right amount of information and text in the right places. Customers do not want to wade through endless fluff before getting to the meat of the proposal. Here is how I recommend that you structure a proposal. The order and flow may vary, but I think a good proposal has these elements:

- Title Page, including the client's logo.

- Table of Contents – very important to enable quick navigation of a large document.

- Introduction – A single page giving an overview of the client's needs and your solution recommendation.

- Executive Summary – A single page giving a thumbnail of each section of the proposal.

- Our Understanding – recapping of client's requirements in your words, to show that YOU understand what THEY need and where they are coming from, in a business sense.

- Our Recommendation – this is where you can paste in the answers to the RFP questions. However, this section needs a "wrapper" which sets up your proposed solution as the one to be selected and explains why that is so.

- Solution Approach – this may or may not be addressed in the

"Our Recommendation" section. This can go into greater depth about your solution than you might in the simple RFP answers, which are often a few sentences long and aimed at answers to very specific technical questions from the client.

- Why Use Our Company? - this is where you explain how great you are

- Project Plan – explain how you intend to implement the solution, including timelines and personnel to be utilized. You may want to add resumes of key project implementers.

- Pricing – breaks out what you what plan to charge.

- Appendices –
  - Depth product detail, if necessary
  - Customer success stories
  - Recent similar projects
  - Client references

Marketing Content and the Concept of "Air Cover"

Sales people, those mythic superstars, believe business is a war and that they are the front-line troops. This notion has some symbolic truth, though anyone who has been through an actual war might find the analogy a bit insulting. Still, those front line solders need "air cover" from you to protect them as they battle the competitors. Like those brave Marines who mounted Mt. Suribachi on Iwo Jima, who needed strafing from P-51s to keep the enemy at bay, your sales people need all types of marketing content to stave off flame-thrower wielding competitors.

Every piece of content, which your salespeople can show to their prospects, is like a 50 caliber round exploding near the foxholes of your competitors. It keeps them from hurting you.

Air cover can take many different forms, though the general rule is the more the better, and the more varied the better. Examples of air cover include:

- Press Links (also known as "clippings" in the old days)

- Collateral

- Technical White Papers

- Marketing White Papers

- Solution Briefs

- Analyst Coverage

- Case Studies (written and video)

- Other marketing content, such as videos, on-demand Webcasts, blog posts

All of the above accrue to the main goal of air cover, which is the sales person's ability to say, "We know what we are doing. People respect us. And, we're prepared and professional enough to have all these materials to show you." As you might intuit, air cover has a lot to do with answering a set of questions which may not have been asked, namely: "Why should we consider your product?", "Has anyone actually used it, or are we your guinea pig?" Note this is not a phenomenon restricted to startups. Established vendors also face credibility challenges when they are introducing something new. Even if you are carrying a bag for a multibillion dollar IT behemoth, if your product is unknown or unproven, you're going to need air cover.

What is the difference, you might be wondering, between a technical white paper and a marketing white paper? Glad you asked. A technical white paper, which we discussed above, goes into depth on a technical topic, explaining numerous details of the customer, which would be of interest to a technical decision-maker. A technical white paper is intended to provide enough clarification on a technical topic to convince a technical decision-maker to consider or prefer your product. In contrast, a marketing white paper is aimed at a business decision-maker and presents the product in a broader business context. It is intended to answer the higher level question, "why is this product right for my business?" The two paper types almost always overlap.

Lead Generation

We've talked about lead generation previously in this book so I won't beat it to death here. What is worth pointing out here, is that lead generation should be seen as part of a bigger sales support function, which marketing performs. All the sales support elements come together when you do lead generation. Whatever the lead generation program is – be it a trade show, email campaign, or Webinar – once the lead is on the hook, you need to be able to deliver a complete sales support package to help the sales team push this lead all the way over the finish line.

CHAPTER 10: IMPLEMENTING THE STRATEGY PART I – THE MARKETING ORGANIZATION

Most of this book has been about how to do marketing for a technology company, so it may seem a little strange to have a chapter dedicated to "doing marketing." However, there is a difference between thinking about what you are going to do and actually making it happen. Now it is time to talk about implementation. I want to pivot into an equally, or perhaps even more important topic, which is, "How you actually make your marketing work." It is one thing to have your messages, materials and lead generation programs ready. It is another to put it all into action in an actual organization, especially a large one. The purpose of this chapter and the rest of the book, is to focus you on approaches to realizing a marketing plan.

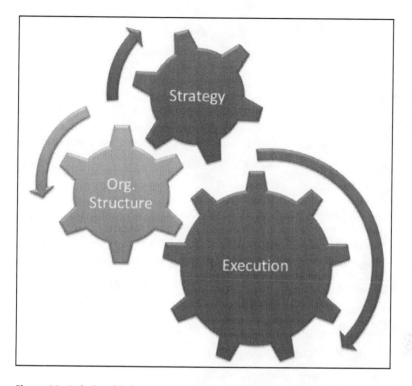

Figure 14 - Relationship between marketing strategy, organizational structure and execution.

When thinking about marketing implementation, a word which comes to mind is "auftragstaktik." I know – you were thinking of that very same word, weren't you? This is an esoteric, German military term, which means "mission command." There is no real English equivalent. "Auftragstaktik" describes how army commanders give their subordinates a clearly defined mission. It is an inclusive term, which refers to the complete set of instructions and resources forces need in order to complete the mission with a certain time frame. The senior level staff is free to focus on the big picture knowing their orders will be executed without their focusing on details. A certain level of knowledge and trust between superiors and subordinates is also implied in "auftragstaktik." Military historians cite good "auftragstaktik" as a reason for the successes of the German army in the field.

We're going to apply some of the principles of "auftragstaktik" to marketing implementation. Marketing is, after all, a blend of strategy, creativity and implementation. You can't have one without the other two. I would make the argument that implementation is perhaps the most important element of marketing. You can have the most brilliant strategy and creative thinking in the world, but if you can't implement, nothing will come from your efforts. Figure 14 shows the relationship between strategy, structure and execution.

A discussion of implementation could take a hundred different directions. A good way to look at this piece is to approach implementation through two essential topics: 1) Marketing organizational structure; and 2) Marketing execution. In "auftragstaktik" terms, the strategy is the high level command, the General's "Occupy this territory" dictum. Organizational structure is about how the army is divided into groups, translated into the various departments and teams in the marketing organization. Execution refers to the field level tactics – guns, grenades, tanks and planes In marketing, execution is about how each team does its work.

Like an army going to war, the marketing group's tactics and organization refer back to the strategy. The three subjects are related. Just as you wouldn't order the Navy to attack Wyoming, you wouldn't task the Web marketing group with creating billboards. Okay, I know some of you are going to be jumping up and down thinking "no!" In fact, you would actually want the Web marketing group to take care of printing billboards. And, you might be right, but you're actually proving my overall point, which is, each organizational unit in marketing will necessarily have some important role to play in strategy execution.

The Shape of the Marketing Organization

Marketing is a task which is almost entirely dependent on **people**. While some aspects of marketing can be automated, virtually every aspect of marketing is devised and executed by people. Even seemingly automatic processes are actually created by people who have to think through what they want to achieve, and then implement their ideas. As a result of marketing's intense reliance on human beings, the marketing organization is of paramount importance in achieving the objectives, which the broader organization requires of the marketing team.

At a high level, the organizational structure will be dictated by size. In this context, you have three options:

- **The small** – This is your basic startup situation with perhaps two or three marketing people covering all of the major marketing work tracks. In a lot of cases, these people will be augmented by contractors and vendors. In the small marketing department, structure is not a big issue, though someone usually has to be in charge (at least in theory.) Marketing people in this type of department handle multiple disciplines.

- **The medium** – In a medium sized marketing department, one team typically handles all the marketing for the company. The medium department may have dozens of people working for it, and multiple teams, but the department is one basic organizational unit. Medium departments usually have one person, or team, for each of the major marketing work areas.

    o Inbound Marketing – a.k.a. lead generation. The inbound group holds lead generation events such as

Webinars, manages trade shows, and conducts the:

- Advertising

- Email marketing

- Content-based marketing

o Product marketing

o Web/Digital marketing

- Website

- Search engine optimization

- Search engine marketing (SEM) or "pay per click"/PPC

- Social media

o Communications, or "comms" or "marcom"

- Public relations

- Analyst relations

- Content-based marketing

o Channel management

o In some cases, two more responsibilities will be added to the marketing department.

- Inside sales

- Business development

A couple of comments: These roles get blurred quite a lot, and responsibilities vary. I.e.. social media might fall under inbound, as could content marketing. And, you may be asking, how is it possible for one person to do all of this? The answer is "yes."

- **The large** – A large company usually has multiple marketing teams placed in different parts of the broader corporate organization. In most cases, these teams work as a matrix, as shown in the organizational chart.

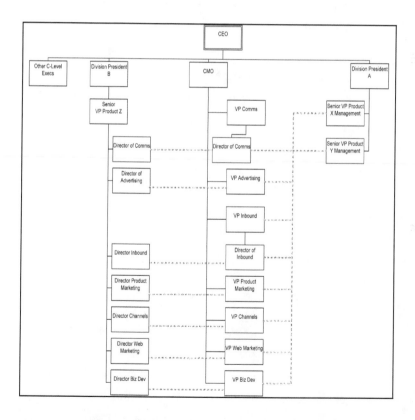

Figure 15 - Organizational chart showing marketing's place in a matrix.

The org chart shown in Figure 15 depicts a fairly typical, if somewhat simplified matrixed marketing organization. In this case, there are two divisions. One has its own dedicated marketing team. The second division has two captive marketing executives who get support from the central, or "corporate" marketing department. Why would the divisions have such different marketing organizational structures? It would depend on the marketing mission of each division. Division B has some intense marketing needs. It has to be on the ground in many different areas, so it requires a marketing staff, which is completely focused on Division B's products and marketing requirements. Division A is in a different business, one in which the marketing is carried out mostly by partners. For example, imagine that Division A makes a part placed in another company's product on an OEM basis. Division A doesn't have a huge marketing task list as a result.

Let's talk about the matrix. The dotted lines in the organization chart refer to informal reporting relationships and collaborations between peers in different groups. In the case of Division A, for example, the Director of Communications reports to the VP of Comms, who reports to the Chief Marketing Officer. He or she is a member of the corporate marketing team. However, on a day-to-day basis, the Director of Comms works mostly with Division A's Senior VP of Product Y Management. This matrixed relationship is effectively one where the Director of Comms is taking direction and doing tasks on assignment from Division A, even though he or she works for the corporate marketing team. Division A could be described as the Director's "Internal client" even though in practical terms, the Division A executive is the boss.

Why would anyone want this type of setup? It seems needlessly complex. Actually, there are many benefits to a matrix though there are some serious challenges with which to contend. One big advantage is that the matrix reduces duplicative functions. With autonomous divisions, you can easily have multiple versions of a complete marketing department in each division. This is based on several fronts. You need a big budget in order to have, for example, a director of public relations for each division when one central person could handle all three. Then, you have the problem of divergent messaging and practices. If three PR people, who are not coordinating, all reach out to the same publication at the same time with three different messages, you're not doing a very good job with PR. And, you are paying triple for the right to do it badly.

From a management perspective, a matrix can also be a good way to keep teams focused on their main missions. If you are a product manager, for example, you have many different product management responsibilities. They are more than enough to absorb your management focus. If you also had to manage marketing people, you might stretch yourself too thin. With a matrix, you can let the marketing department manage the marketers, who provide service to your team. It is as though you were working with an outside vendor who happens to be inside your same company.

The Compound Matrix

Tolstoy wrote *"Every unhappy family is unhappy in its own way."* If only Tolstoy could have seen today's extended, globally matrixed marketing organizations, I think we'd be reading a thousand page tome about the utter tragedy of it all. Our matrix depicted in figure 15 is only **one-dimensional**. In reality, at a global technology company, the marketing matrix can get a lot more complicated.

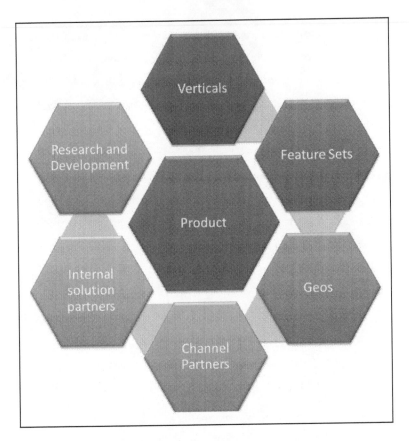

Figure 16 - The parts of the marketing matrix.

Figure 16 attempts to show the six potentially additional dimensions, which may be a part of a standard matrixed marketing organization. Briefly, you have the following groups connected, (though usually not reporting to) to the core product marketing team:

- **Verticals** – Some companies like to market by vertical, so you'll have a group. which for example, focuses on marketing to the automotive industry, telecoms and government.

- **Feature sets** – In some cases, a product with multiple feature sets will have a separate team for each major feature. This was the case with Microsoft SharePoint, where one team handled search and another focused on content management.

- **Geos** – Any large company will have different geographic marketing teams. The scope of the matrix will depend on the size of the geographical territory. Generally, smaller markets – both within the US and abroad – will have one marketing team handling all of a company's products. Thus, (purely as an illustration and not as revealing any facts) Microsoft's marketing team in Portugal might handle the entire Office, Windows, and server product sets. In the UK, in contrast, which is a bigger market, there might be a dedicated Office marketing team, a Windows team, and so on. Inside the US, the same structure will emerge. The New York metro area will likely have numerous product specific local market teams, while South Dakota will have one team (or maybe even just one person!) who handles the entire line.

- **Channel partners** – Some channel partners are detached 3rd parties while others are so big and influential, they can effectively be an <u>additional</u> marketing team. There is a reason they call Windows-based PCs "WinTel Machines" – this directly refers to the close connection between Microsoft and Intel. If a product has a special channel, the product marketing team will be matrixed to the channel partners' marketing organization to some extent.

- **Internal solution partners** – If your company sells solutions in addition to products, you may find your product matrixed to one or more solution groups. This is the case even if your company offers only guidance on solutions to partners who actually do the solution selling. For example, if you're in the ERP business, you may have a unit which focuses on mobile ERP. This group will focus on making sure your ERP product is compatible with various mobile devices and hand-held computing equipment, such as bar-code scanners.

- **Research and Development** – R&D runs the gamut as far as matrixed marketing organizations go, but generally speaking, you will have some connection points with groups which conduct customer research and develop new product concepts.

All of these groups participate in marketing. They have input on what you are doing and will need materials, input and feedback from you. It can be a messy setup with numerous groups, each with different management, goals and timelines, all trying to coordinate their activities. And - this just keeps getting better doesn't it? - in a very large company, for example, the top 10 largest technology companies in the world, you will have multiple versions of each matrix functioning within each major business unit. The organization chart will look something like figure 17, shown below.

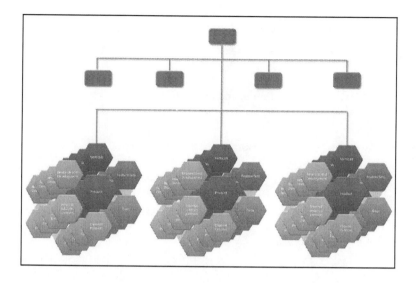

Figure 17 - The multi-matrix large organization.

Matching Business Strategy to Marketing Organization, Priorities and Control

Most companies which have the multi-layered matrix shown in [Figure 17] try to match the matrix to their marketing strategy. But, wow - what a mess! And just to make it even more insane, add in the constant churn of people coming and going from positions. It is a wonder that anything ever gets done at all. How does it work? In practical terms, matching the matrix to the marketing strategy means creating priorities and emphasis, by handing control to the most strategically important people and teams in the matrix. Without some type of emphasis, the compound matrix will not function well. And, indeed, sometimes these complex organizations don't run very effectively, even if there is a strategy dictating who is in charge.

A company might be solution-centric or industry-centric. In an industry-centric company, the industry vertical group gets the authority to make the other groups do what they want, more or less. There might also be horizontal market segments, which receive priority. Alternatively, the matrix can be managed using a schedule. You can organize product marketing into scheduled waves of activity. This is Microsoft's tactic, with "release waves" of product families, such as Office, occurring at preset three year intervals. The calendar dictates much activity which occurs across dozens of individual groups.

The real question with a compound matrix organization is "Who owns the business?" Some person or group has to be in the lead or the matrix will not work. The entity which owns the business sets the agenda, to some degree, of the other elements of the matrix. A lot of the time, the business owner is the product manager. For example, at Microsoft, there is the "Information Worker Product Management Group," which is responsible for the overall business of Microsoft Office. The business owner is responsible for coordinating with the other elements of the matrix to make the business move in the desired direction. In some cases the business owner will determine the budget allocation for other matrix elements, though just as often, the units are independently-funded and must agree to work together on a cooperative basis.

It isn't easy to get a separate business team, which you do not control, through budget, to agree to do what you want them to do. This is where leadership comes into play. Or not. When there is strong leadership at the top, different pieces of the matrix are able to join forces, get together, and agree on a plan which will play to the dominant strategy. For example, if the company has been pushing horizontal product features decides to shift to a vertical focus, the senior management needs to get consensus amongst the matrix unit leaders to cooperate by making vertical markets the priority. There is usually a lot of push and pull leading to compromise. Ideally, the negotiation of priority results in an optimal deployment of all the matrixed resources. Of course, this is not always the case. Often, the matrix just grinds along, each part doing what it does, and marketing happens in the process. Chaos is not the best way to do things, but like those mediocre but plentiful Sherman Tanks rolling off the ships in Normandy in 1944, a lot of movement in the right direction will achieve some strategic goals.

Organizational Puzzles

Where does marketing fit in an organization? For example, should marketing report to sales? If you ask me (and let's face it, if you're reading this, you are asking me) I think marketing should not report to sales. Many companies have a person called "VP of Sales and Marketing." This is, in my view, a mistake. This person is invariably a sales professional who most probably lacks the knowledge or time to manage marketing effectively. When you have marketing report to sales in this way, you're relegating marketing to a second tier status.

If you do find yourself in charge of marketing at a company where you report to sales, my suggestion is to work hard on negotiating your autonomy. This may be easier said than done, yet definitely necessary if you want to avoid being a sales doormat. For instance, as a marketer, you must take a relatively long term view of the marketing process. Yes, you need to generate leads with immediate business potential, but, you also have to work on building the type of sustainable credibility and repeated touch points, which will lead to sustained marketing success. A sales manager may not see things the way you do. I realize I'm being grossly unfair and generalizing here, but if you think about the conflicting incentives involved you'll see what I mean. The sales manager usually has a short term set of goals, perhaps stretching from the nearest quarter to the end of the fiscal year. This is about as far as he or she is going to think about approving budget for marketing efforts. After this, said sales manager may be history anyway… It can be time for a fight if you want to pursue the longer term, or perhaps more subjective ROI programs you know the company needs.

The Right Place for Business Development

What about business development? Where do marketing and business development fit within an organization. Like everything else in this discussion, it depends. But of course, I have an opinion on the subject. Biz dev is a function which varies from company to company, but the focus is mostly about arranging partnerships with other businesses, which will resell or facilitate the sale of your product. It is probably a closer relative to sales than it is to marketing, but the disciplines overlap. As a result, marketing sometimes get parked under biz dev. The converse is also true. Biz dev can get slotted within the marketing department. Sometimes, marketing and biz dev both report to sales.

There is no ideal solution to this, but in my experience, biz dev should be autonomous or largely left alone within the organizational unit which houses it. The reasons for this preference stem from a recognition that biz dev is inherently different from sales and marketing, even though biz dev bears a superficial resemblance to them. Biz dev should be free from the quantitative time pressure of sales as well as from the broader mandates of marketing. Of course, biz dev, marketing and sales all need to align strategically, but biz dev should be free to pursue its own agenda. At the same time, it is critical for sales and marketing – as well as Product Development - to be at arm's length from biz dev's agenda.

Biz dev is in the "maybe" business. Like a shopper who wonders what a dress in the store window will look like on her, the biz dev executive looks at many potential partners and tries to find a profitable business fit. If you don't like the analogy, think "kissing frogs." Biz dev has to kiss a lot of frogs to see if any potential partner is going to turn into Prince Charming. This is all fine, but frog kissing may lead to a lot of wasted cycles in marketing, if there is not a healthy distance between the two.

Consider the following scenario: the biz dev person gets excited by the idea of partnering with company X as a reseller. With a partnership in hand (perhaps informal, perhaps contractual, though it really makes no difference in practical terms) he leans on marketing to create collateral, presentations, press releases, sales training materials and white papers, to support the new partnership. The process is time consuming. It may also require stretching existing messaging and value propositions to fit the partner's go-to-market strategy. All of this work and distortion will be worth it, if the partnership produces revenue. If the partnership doesn't perform, and most of them don't, a lot of time will have been wasted. Plus, there is an opportunity cost. Other marketing didn't get done while you were being pushed (and rushed, usually, as well) to get the partnership marketing materials ready. For this reason, strive for some balance in the biz dev-marketing relationship, as well as some executive oversight, which would help assign priorities to biz dev's requirements.

Biz dev can also tax engineering resources if it is not managed well. I don't mean to dump on biz dev. I've been in the role myself a few times, so what I have to say comes from experience on both sides of the issue. What can happen though, is when biz dev gets wind of a potential partnership, it presses engineering for modifications or new features, which the partner wants. These may or may not be on the roadmap and they may or may not be trivial. If they are non-trivial and unplanned, someone needs to take the leadership role and decide whether the changes are truly warranted. For example, let's say your software company has an opportunity to resell its application through a major social network. Sounds great! And, maybe it is. But, creating the APIs and coding for functionality to make it happen could be a major project. If the work is going to be done on spec, it is a very serious judgment call as to whether it should be undertaken. Marketing may be called to join in these discussions. What do you think of this partnership? Is it worth spending resources on? Or, more accurately, is it worth diverting resources from other work to get this done? As the master of strategy, which now you surely are after reading this book, you will undoubtedly be able to offer brilliant advice.

Web Marketing and Social Media

Where does Web marketing fit in the marketing organization? How about social media? There is definitely more than one correct answer to each of these questions. The issue, though, is one of boundaries. Web marketing and social media, are distinct disciplines with clearly delineated work tracks. For example, building and maintaining the Website is a Web marketing activity. As such, it could easily justify a standalone organizational unit for Web Marketing. A VP or Director level manager could be assigned all Web marketing tasks. At the same time, Web marketing cuts across nearly every single aspect of marketing and sales.

Consider, for example, search engine optimization (SEO). This is a purely Web marketing activity, at least in technical terms. However, SEO is actually a profound focal point for all marketing and communications work. SEO drives the question, "What will people be thinking about when they are looking for a company like ours?" This is not a Web marketing issue alone; this is a big, high-level question, which needs to be answered by many different voices inside marketing and beyond.

Structurally, Web marketing should be a matrix within the marketing group. Whoever runs Web marketing should plan to reach out to many different people and teams. Web marketing works best when it incorporates the goals and strategies of the complete marketing effort. Social media is similar. New as it is, social media marketing is still the province of the young, the special, and the different. This is not necessarily a bad thing, but as a lot of marketers are finding with social media, to get any type of payback from the process, it has to be grounded in marketing basics. Essentially, social media is a form of public relations (i.e. media relations). It is also a form of lead generation and CRM. It is sometimes an end unto itself, but it is not the main purpose of social media. Like Web marketing, social media should try to matrix itself within marketing and work to integrate broader marketing messages and objectives into its campaigns.

Contractors and Outsourcing

Who should actually work for your marketing department and who should be hired as a contractor? Which work should be assigned to vendors versus kept in house? The quick answer is, it will depend on your budget. If you can afford full time people, hire them. If you need to contract out certain work due to budget constraints, then this is what you'll do. Not always. The contract vs. hire question affects large and small marketing organizations alike. For very small marketing teams, such as you would find at a startup, the issue may be forced. At wealthier companies, this would be more a blend of strategic and corporate HR policies. The underlying issues, however, are always the same.

The contract vs. hire choice revolves around two basic questions. First, what are the core strengths and mandates of the department? These should guide hiring. You want to hire people with skills and experience, which are most closely aligned with the department's prime mission. Second, how do you define value for marketing budget spent?

For this second point, consider the following: hiring vs. contracting decision. Let's say your department has an unmet need for both public relations and search engine optimization. You want to kick off campaigns in both areas but you lack the staff to get the work done. One solution would be to hire someone who could do both tasks. Such a person would have to be adept at both PR and SEO. Even though these two skillsets are nowhere near as far apart as they used to be, they are still quite distinct. Whomever you hire will likely be slightly less effective at each skill than a dedicated resource would be. You can't afford to hire two people, however. You could contract out SEO and PR and get a better result in each category. Your spend might be higher, but so would your value.

Imagine you could hire a full time PR and SEO person for $75,000 a year, or $90,000 with benefits and taxes included. In contrast, what would it cost you to find a contractor for each? If you paid two contractors a rate of $60 per hour each for 20 hours a week (1000 hours a year), your cost would be $120,000. It would be $30,000 more, yet probably worth it.v Where you have to be careful though, is with vendors who substitute dedicated personnel. You might end up paying $15,000 a month for PR and $5000 a month for SEO. Now you're paying $240,000 and the value received is probably about the same as with contractors. It may be better, of course, and you might get better accountability from a vendor in comparison to a lone contractor, but you have to do the math and weigh what you really expect to gain from the situation.

Chapter 11: Implementing the Strategy Part II – Planning and Budgeting

Marketing execution is about the realization of strategy. Strategy begets objectives. The attainment of objectives requires planning and execution. All four elements – strategy, objectives, plan and execution, must be in alignment for marketing to work. Surely, there are many ways to bring about this alignment, but one method I have seen work quite well, is an approach known as the "Cascading Scorecard."

Cascading Commitments and Scorecards

Scorecarding is an approach to management which requires people to be evaluated, and evaluate themselves, using simple and periodic performance indicators. The specifics of scorecarding vary greatly, but in general, an individual scorecard will contain Hi/Medium/Low type of scores for specific work objectives over a quarter or a year. At Microsoft, where I first became familiar with this technique, each employee needed to make commitments to his or her manager for the coming year. The employee's ability to achieve the commitment would be graded on the scorecard. For example, I made a commitment to generate 1,000 pieces of news coverage for SharePoint. This became my goal. By the end of the year, we had 800 articles. Not bad, but it didn't meet or exceed my commitment. I gave myself a yellow (medium score) on my scorecard for SharePoint coverage. If I had gotten 200 articles, I would have given myself a red, for low score. Green is reserved for meeting or exceeding goals. A simple sample scorecard is shown below in Table 17.

Table 17 - Sample Scorecard

Commitment	Achieved		Eval	Comment
500 white paper downloads	300	⬤	Failed	Need to do better with keyword selection
50 articles and press mentions	55	●	Exceeded	Working with partners helped boost coverage
Manage special team	Done	⬤	Met	
10 press releases	9	⬤	Met	Got pushed aside by bigger announcement from another department

In a commitment-based organization such as Microsoft, there is a tendency for commitments to "cascade" from the top leadership down to department heads and individuals. In 2008, Jeff Raikes, President of Microsoft Business Division, made a personal commitment on his scorecard to Steve Ballmer that PerformancePoint Server, the business intelligence (BI) product, would rank in the Gartner BI Leader's Quadrant. Once he made this personal commitment and prepared to stand by the scorecard results to his boss, a lot of people working for him got busy to make it happen. If you looked at the commitments and scorecards of the department heads working for Raikes in that year, they contained objectives which would accrue to the achievement of the leadership quadrant.

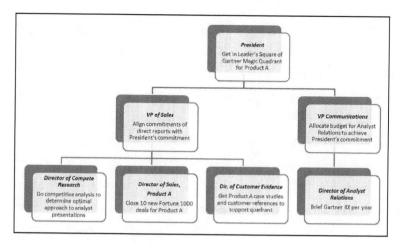

Figure 18 - Example of cascading scorecard.

Figure 18 shows how commitments cascade from senior management. In this generic example, inspired by the Jeff Raikes case, the President's personal commitment to get a product on to the leader's square of the Magic Quadrant flows to two VPs reporting to him or her. The VP of Communications who oversees Analyst Relations, aligns his or her commitments with the President's, and arranges for the Director of Analyst Relations to have the resources to realize the Magic Quadrant goal. The Director also has the same commitment of getting the product onto the leader's square. The VP of Sales also aligns commitments to help the President with the goal. He or she discusses the President's commitment with several direct reports and asks them to make specific commitments, which support the Magic Quadrant. These direct reports then confer with the Director of Analyst Relations who has three specific needs, which these people would hopefully fulfill: More deals for the product in question, more case studies and client references, and additional competitive analysis. These requests become commitments for the Director of Compete Research, Director of Sales for the product, and the Director of Customer Evidence.

You might wonder why all of this discussion and committing is necessary to achieve a fairly simple objective such as getting onto the leader's quadrant at Gartner. It is of course possible to have a completely top-down directive process, where the President instructs each person for exactly what is needed to achieve the goal. In some cases this is precisely what happens. However, in a large matrixed and decentralized organization, the cascading commitment technique enables the most effective approach to realizing a strategic goal. In this example, the President has determined that Product A is a key strategic product for the company. For this reason, he or she wants it to be considered a <u>leader</u> by Gartner. This will require a high level of focus and resource allocation, which not every product can receive.

Each manager reporting to the President is given flexibility and discretion in aligning with the President's commitment. The President is saying, in effect, "You can do whatever you want, but pay attention to my commitment and do what you consider best to make it happen." The manager would be a fool to ignore the President's personal commitment. He will make sure to support it. But, he will support it in a way which makes sense to him, with his specific resources and personnel. The underlying issue is that each manager and team member in an organization has a limited amount of time and resources to accomplish any set of tasks in a given year. The commitment process asks, basically, if you were to do just 5 or 10 things this year, what would they be? Which are the most critical? Focus on those.

Cascading commitments work well when they are aligned with effective organizational leadership. They can help cultivate leadership and independent thinking in an organization. When people get too much top-down direct instruction, they tend to switch off their brains. The opposite is true when they have to figure out for themselves the best way to help realize a company strategy. However, a matrix structure can make the commitment process messy and shield people from accountability. Additionally, a cascading commitment can lead a group of people to fall into lockstep behind a bad idea. Good leadership in an organization will try to encourage independent thinking and productive questioning of goals, while motivating people to realize the commitments which the senior executives have made.

Planning

The scorecard measures the results of execution, as guided by a marketing plan. I started with a description of the scorecard even though it comes later in the process, because the scorecard (or comparable mechanism) is essential in understanding your goals, and how you will be evaluated on execution before you start planning. It is possible to plan without thinking this through, but you may be unpleasantly surprised by the result. And, you need to pay attention to the cascading commitments coming down from above. They exist even if your company doesn't officially have this policy. Whether or not your boss, or her boss's boss has a scorecard, there will still be high level objectives, which you will be expected to help meet.

Marketing plans vary in their form and length. Whatever their shape, though, a marketing plan must contain the following elements:

- High-level strategy and objectives

- Objectives by focus area (e.g., Web or Lead Generation)

- A strategy for attaining those objectives

- A tactical plan for executing the strategy

- What is going to happen

- Who is going to do it

- Regular success metrics across the period of time covered by the plan

Optional elements of a marketing plan

- Competitive analysis

- Market analysis

- Evaluation of results from previous planning periods

A high-level plan usually contains major goals for market share and revenue growth. In addition, there is often a goal of increasing brand awareness or making other gains in "customer audience mind share."

Table 18 – High level marketing plan summary.

High Level Plan Summary				
Focus Area	Objectives	Strategies	Tactics	Tactical Success Metrics
Revenue and Market Share	• 10% increase in market share • 15% increase in revenue	• Increase direct sales • Expand product line • Box out competition using solutions in cross functional areas • Leverage the channel	• Launch new SKUs • Launch new multi-SKU products • Increase number of channel partners • Increase sales per channel partner • Demand generation	• 5 new SKUs launched • 3 new solutions launched • Added 10 new partners • Grew partner revenue 20% per partner • 50,000 new prospects added to database • 1,000 major deals added to sales pipeline
Awareness	• 25% increase in unaided product awareness • 25% increase in number of people who put Product X in top 3 candidates for procurement	• Influence the influencers – media, analysts, key bloggers	• Analyst relations push • Content marketing campaigns • Media relations push • Presence at industry events	• Leader in in Gartner Magic Quadrant for Product X • 500 mentions in media • 10 direct articles and/or bylines • 5 conference keynotes

The high-level plan in Table 18 begets the tactical plans from which we work day-to-day. Major objectives are realized through numerous dependent tactical steps. Figure 19 below shows the flow of strategy from major focus areas to tactical areas and smaller-scale objectives. For example, as part of the strategic goal of increasing unaided awareness by 25%, there is a tactical success metric of getting 500 mentions in the media. Attaining this metric will depend on numerous other tactical steps, each with their own metric: to get 500 media mentions, the PR component of the overall marketing plan needs to break the goal into manageable chunks and determine a course of action to get the desired coverage. Each chunk of activity will then have its own success metric.

Figure 19 - The Flow of activity from business strategy through marketing execution and tactics.

Table 19 below shows an excerpt from the detailed marketing plan, which supports the high-level strategy and plan. In this case, the public relations objective of 500 media mentions is to be achieved through a three-part strategy. Needless to say, 500 media mentions won't just happen on their own, nor will you get them through random PR activity. A goal of this size can only be achieved through careful planning and execution of a distinct tactical plan. In this case, the company will use a combination of direct story pitches to media outlets, media outreach related to product launches as well partner media collaboration to fulfill the objective. Table 19 summarizes how it works. For each strategy, there will be a related tactical plan. The detailed plan puts out three strategies for getting press coverage. Twenty direct story pitches - where the company will solicit coverage from publications - are planned with the goal of getting 100 media mentions. The firm will leverage product launches with 10 corporate press releases with the aim of getting 200 mentions and so forth. A "reach goal" is set out as well, with the ambitious vision of getting an in-depth profile of the company in a major business publication.

Table 19 – Setting goals based on strategy for an area of the marketing plan.

Focus Area	Objective	Strategy	Tactics	Success Metrics
Public Relations	500 mentions in media	Direct story pitches	20 story pitches	100 mentions Reach goal: 1 in-depth profile in tier 1 business publication
		Leverage product launches	10 corporate press releases	200 mentions
		Working with partners helped boost coverage	40 partner press releases	200 mentions

Plan Review

The marketing plan exists mostly for your own use in getting your work done and making sure that you are allocating effort and resources against important goals. However, the plan can also very much be a consensus piece, which you can use to achieve buy-in from key internal stakeholders. The mode of most senior managers is "What have you done for me lately?" The *Plan* is your answer. "Here is what I've done/doing/will do for you." And, if you give senior leadership the opportunity to look at your plan and comment on it before you put it into action, you will have an easier time explaining what you've done for them lately.

In some companies, a marketing plan review is built into the operating process of the business. You are asked to prepare a draft plan and then have it appraised by affected stakeholders. Their input will influence revisions and a final plan for execution. For example, you may be asked to present your plan for comment to engineering and sales before locking it. This makes sense because the way you do marketing will affect the commercial success of a product they are building.

In many cases, this process is scheduled into the calendar. If your fiscal year starts January 1, you will be required to present a marketing plan for review by other departments around October. You will then have some pre-determined time period to respond to comments, re-circulate a revised draft, etc.

Plan review ranges from a formality to a true consultative process, which works across the organizational matrix. If you don't know where you stand, my suggestion is to approach the process informally. You can suggest that your various colleagues look at your plan and give you feedback. You may get nothing for your efforts. I've had this experience – showing a plan and feeling as if I'd just dropped a feather in the Grand Canyon and expected to hear an echo. Tumbleweeds... Crickets... However, you've done the right thing. You've reached out and asked people who are affected by what you do to comment on your plans. This is not just about covering your behind. People want to be consulted, even if they don't react effusively.

Matching Budget to Objectives

As you finalize your plan, your attention will inevitably pivot to budget. A plan has to translate into a budget. Truth is, you've probably worked out a rough budget before you started your plan. Because...they go together, right? You can't plan on exhibiting at 25 trade shows at $20,000 a pop if your total trade show budget is $10,000. This sounds obvious, but I wouldn't point it out if I hadn't lived through a few situations where marketers' planning ideas were out of alignment with financial reality.

Figure 20 - The budget reality check process.

Budgeting is about making choices. Figure 20 above shows the healthy version of the budget thought process. You think about what you might get in terms of budget. You lay out your wish list and then see how the budget falls out. Depending on what you can get, you plan accordingly. In the example shown above, you might have to pick your four top trade shows if this is all that your budget allows, even though you wanted ten in the beginning. Of course, you could try to drop your per-show budget to $10K and do all the shows. However, do not short-change yourself in other ways. There is a cost for appearing cheap.

Ready for a serious reality check? Here goes: Marketing budgets are always limited. Whoa? Is this a huge news flash? It shouldn't be. If you work for a cash-strapped startup, this will not be a major insight. When you are scrambling to afford people who actually write code, your frilly marketing stuff is going to look like a pretty low priority. You'll be begging for money. But what if you are ensconced at a major player with endless bucks? Guess what? You still have to beg for money. The reason is there will always be something better to do with the money – or at least that's what people think. This is true inside and out of marketing. Should your company spend a billion dollars on marketing, or $900 million? Should $100 million go to something else? A lot of executives in other departments are probably screaming for the $100 million, so you had better have a very good idea of what you are going to do with it.

Inside marketing, how should you spend your billion? (You wish you had this problem, right? But you know… this is painful no matter how much or little you have.) How much should you allocate to brand advertising, to public relations, social media, Internet marketing and so forth? Your priorities and allocations will depend on your objectives and plan. The budget should flow from the plan.

Table 20 – Budget wish list, "ask" vs. "get."

Category	Wish List	Ask for Budget	Granted	Percent	Decision	Final	Percent
Trade shows	20 shows	$20,000 each $400,000 ask	$100,000	43%	Raise	$120,000	52%
Email Marketing	50 mailings	$2,000 each $100,000 ask	$50,000	22%	Reduce	$30,000	13%
Pay-per-Click		$100,000 ask	$20,000	9%	Stay same	$20,000	9%
Public Relations	2 person agency team	$30,000/month $360,000 ask	$60,000	26%	Stay same	$60,000	26%
Total		$960,000	$230,000	100%		$230,000	100%

Table 20, shown above, is a simplified budget worksheet. The wish list contains all the things you might want to be able to do to achieve your objectives. You want to do 20 trade shows and 50 email campaigns. Your total ask is almost a million dollars. But, in today's economy, you are in for a rude shock when your CEO says, "You are going to have to make do with less than a quarter million. " Welcome to venture-backed technology marketing (or big company marketing, depending on where you work.) So, what can you do? You are given a set of numbers to work with: $100,000 for trade shows, not $400,000; $60,000 for PR, not $360,000. Will those do? Go back to your objectives and plan. You may need to reallocate. You may decide to shift $20,000 away from email marketing and do one more trade show.

This process may occur over several iterations. For one thing, you may want to ask is for more money. Asking for 960 and getting 230 is a bit harsh. Maybe your CEO will crank you up to 500 grand if you are persuasive. The allocation game will still continue. How much do you want to spend on each category? It depends on your objectives. This process will force you to compare your objectives and determine which ones are really worth the investment. In this case, you're deciding that one more trade show is more important than ten email campaigns. You may also need to change your objectives as the budget process goes through its phases If you were planning on getting a thousand leads from 20 trade shows, you are not likely to get the same thousand with six shows. Your goal will have to be revised downward.

If you are reallocating by adding to budgets, you need to be aware of the law of diminishing returns. Sometimes adding to a budget won't get you more of the results you seek. Public relations and analyst relations are great examples of this phenomenon. Analyst coverage is a great marketing asset, so there can be a temptation to pump a ton of money into it. At a certain level of spending, this works. Five million dollars invested in AR is better than one million. You get more consults, more attention, and more traction. However, what if you wanted to spend a hundred million on AR? (We all should have this problem, right? But, this is a serious issue at very big companies.) Given that real analysts can't be bought, a big portion of the hundred million will be wasted. I don't know if it is even possible to spend a hundred million on Gartner and Forrester. I'm sure they could find a way, but you would be facing diminishing returns.

Realistically, the scorecard setting, planning, and budget process happens all at the same time. Even in companies where the process is formal and highly scheduled, there is a subjective process of collaboration on planning. Objectives and priorities shift as strategies evolve. Money allocated to marketing rises and falls. Your job is to stay on top of all of this and get your department the best possible budget for the plan.

Who Will Do the Work?

As your plan and budget take shape, the inevitable question will arise: Who is actually going to do all this work? Someone other than you, right? Of course! To be serious for a minute, it is probable that there will be more work than a team of full-time employees can handle. You have three choices to tackle the normal overflow. You can hire more people. You can bring in contractors. You can outsource to vendors. You can do all three, as well. Each approach has its good and bad points.

- Hiring more full time employees (FTEs) – this is usually hard to do, for many reasons. For one thing, most companies don't like adding costly overhead. Full-time people are expensive and long term. It can be difficult to find the right people. If you need work done quickly, adding FTEs is not the right way to go.

- Contractors can be great – You bring them in. They do the work. You pay them. They move on to their next gig. What could be bad about this scenario? Contractors are problematic for a couple of reasons. They develop the skills you need and then they disappear with all their new found knowledge. It might take some time for them to ramp up to being productive, and your investment in their training is wasted. There can also be friction between FTEs and contractors, with resentment over benefits and pay. It is not always healthy to have two tiers of employees.

- Vending work out to other companies – This is often your only choice for certain tasks, as would be the case with an advertising agency or video production. In some cases, it will make sense to hire out the work. A lot of the time, though, you will end up overpaying for services more easily done by in-house contractors.

You will likely use all three approaches to getting the work done. However, there is a way to determine what to keep internal with FTEs, what to assign to contractors, and what to vend out. The main question you want to ask yourself is what type of marketing team do you want to have? What are the core skills that you want to have for the long-term? Those are the areas where you want to hire FTEs. For example, if you are a direct marketing organization, then you will want FTEs who have extensive experience with direct marketing. Contractors can handle non-core work, such as print production. List management and analysis - that is for FTEs. If you understand what your team's core mission is all about, here is where you fight for FTEs and work hard to find the right people.

Chapter 12: Implementing the Strategy Part III – Into Action

The time has come. You have your plan and structure. It is time to execute. Some of you may think, "What is such a big deal about that?" You have a plan. Go and do it, right? Yes and no. Yes, you show up every day and work from the plan that you wrote and the objectives that you set. At some level, it is just about that simple. Sometimes it's not.

Eating the Elephant

How do you eat an elephant? One bite at a time… This saying could describe the B2B technology marketing execution process. You have a huge job. You need to accomplish certain goals within a defined period of time. How do you get it done? Answer: Eat the elephant one bite at a time. There are many different ways of going about marketing execution. I will share with you some techniques and tools which have worked for me in marketing contexts ranging from one-person shops to multi-billion dollar marketing departments.

The Walking Deck

I have a tendency to show up at my office and freak out about a multitude of tasks which are competing for my brain space. I have developed a marketing execution tool which helps me manage multiple work tracks. The multi-track execution tool is a PowerPoint Deck. It is easy to project on a screen during marketing team meetings. In Microsoft-speak, it might be called a "walking deck" because it "walks" from conference room to conference room. But there is no reason it has to be a deck. It can be anything you feel comfortable using. The principles are the same no matter whether you use a legal pad or a custom-built application. The multi-track tool needs:

- A summary of major work tracks and tasks

- A breakout of work track detail

- Period-specific objectives aligned with current work activities

Table 21 – A sample "top sheet" or "to do" list for a marketing work track.

Track	Major Current Tasks		Status/Comment
Lead Generation	• GraphicCollab conference in June • "Image Management" Webinar planned for July 8th		• Must lock down trade show choices • Set Webinar production meeting rhythm
Brand	Graphic style refresh and guide		Need to create production schedule (work with agency)
Advertising	Collab Magazine - Year-long print campaign – refresh ad copy for August issue		
Email	• Update newsletter template • List buys: Look at art director selections		
PR	• Press release announcing v 2.1 • Byline article on image management – complete by 7/15 for deadline at Image Magazine		
Content	Digital asset security whitepaper – due 8/1		
Web	Update copy on product page for v 2.1 Review PPC results and determine Q3 plan		
Case studies	**Written** AllCorp P&G	**Video** P&G	
Partner/Other	Adobe – need to register officially for partner status		Budget approval required
Product Marketing	Create updated data sheet for v 2.1		

Table 21 is an example of a summary or top sheet, for the multi-track marketing execution tool. This is basically a "to do" list, but it is intended to keep you organized and focused on the work tracks which matter. It is certainly possible that you don't have a problem staying organized and focused, but we marketing types tend to be distractible, so I recommend it. Your top sheet will likely change on a regular basis.

Everyone's approach to managing the recurring changes will vary. I personally create a new top sheet every week. You might want to do it daily. I like to print my top sheet out so I can mark it up and make comments. At the end of the week, the page is a jumble of scribbles, which I then decode as I update the sheet for the coming week. If you are using a digital "sheet" such as Microsoft Office OneNote, this will be less of an issue, though the hard part is usually finding the discipline to keep the sheet maintained, regardless of the form factor.

Table 22 – Work track and goals summary slide sample.

Lead Generation				
Task Category	**To Do**	**Owner**	**Critical Dates**	**Other Tasks/Notes**
Advertising	Put QR code into print ad – link to mobile landing page	HB	Art due 7/1	Need to redefine lead qualification process in Salesforce.com.
Email Marketing	Create topics for next 5 sends	SR	Do by 6/5	Plan December sales meeting
Webcasts	"Image Management" Webinar	SR	6/1 – send invites	
Events	GraphicCollab conference	HB	Exhib forms due 6/2	

Objectives					
	Q1	Q2	Q3	Q4	Year Total
Total Leads - Objective	1000	1000	1200	800	4000
Total Leads – Actual	891				891
Fortune 500 leads - Objective	50	50	60	40	200
Fortune 500 leads - Actual	44				44

I like to follow the top sheet with a series of detail sheets, or slides. The example, shown above in Table 22, tracks activities and results for lead generation. The detail sheet is meant to be a day-to-day guide to priorities in certain focus areas. The sheet is partially redundant with the top sheet, but I like to have a detail sheet to keep me aware of the bigger picture. And, the detail sheet is where you put everything – all the deadlines and tasks, which are going on – so that nothing is forgotten or overlooked. Each task has an owner, so you can assign work and build accountability. The detail sheet becomes a way for team members to reach consensus on who is doing what and when a task is supposed to be finished. I also like to put the objectives onto the detail sheet so I can track how I'm doing according to plan at any time.

The Marketing Calendar

A marketing calendar is an ideal companion for the walking deck. I don't think I need to tell you how to fill out a calendar; but, my suggested format below might give you some practical ideas. The figure shows a quarterly calendar which breaks down marketing activities according to the major work tracks for each quarter. The quarterly view is a great way to give yourself, your team, and other stakeholders an overview of how you plan to conduct marketing over the course of the year.

Table 23 – Year at a glance work plan summary.

Work Stream	Category	Q1	Q2	Q3	Q4
Lead Generation	Trade show	• Digital Image Show • Content Management Summit	DigiCon West	GraphicCollab	• DreamForce • DigiCon East
	Email	Fortune 1000 campaigns	Government sector campaigns	Reseller outreach	Fortune 1000 Part II
	Webinars	Gartner guest speaker	Customer case TBD	Customer case TBD	Forrester guest speaker
Product Marketing		V 1 launch		1.1 upgrade release	
Partner Marketing			Partner meeting		Regional partner meetings
Comms/Content/ Branding		*Digital Image* magazine top 10 products issue	Content campaign - Part I	Content campaign - Part II	*Digital Image* magazine end of year wrap up issue
Web Marketing	Website		Site refresh	Roll out partner portal	
	Pay Per Click (SEM)	Pause campaign & review prior year results	Revamp and Re-launch	Add: 2nd keyword category ("Document management")	Add: 3rd keyword category (Digital Asset Management DAM)

The calendar is also a great budget and planning tool, as it forces you to map out the main activities you plan to undertake in each work track for the full year. Table 23 shows an example of a quarterly calendar for marketing. You may find, as you calendar all the tradeshows and events you want to do, that you haven't budgeted adequately for all of them. Should you cut events or some other activity to pay for those events? The calendar can provide a helpful forcing function. Similarly, the calendar can help you see how your staff will be utilized. You might notice that Q2 has your team scheduled to run an email campaign, hold a partner meeting, run a content campaign, refresh the Website and re-launch the PPC campaign all at the same time. Perhaps you will need some supplementary help at that time. The calendar provides a catalyst for thinking through your resource needs.

The quarterly calendar is coarse-grained. You will have to create some type of weekly or monthly calendar to see how things will play out in real time. I used to take a regular wall calendar, tear out the pages and tape them up in a 12-month row all around my office. I would then write specific dates for activities and deadlines in different colors to reflect the work track. Red was for trade shows, blue for PR, green for AR, etc. The cadence of work and planning would then flow accordingly.

Meetings and Team Process

Do you hate meetings? I do, but they are a necessity in marketing. Yes, there are some marketing departments which function well without many meetings. Everyone is a total professional, and knows what is expected of them, and follows the plan. Voila! It all just gets done. Chances are, in those departments where they don't meet too often, there is not a lot of innovation or change going on. They are probably doing the same things they did last year, and the year before that. In any marketing situations I've ever found myself, there is a non-stop swirl of new ideas, testing new approaches to marketing, and figuring out who is going to do what. Keeping this sort of marketing organized requires meetings.

The challenge is to hold enough meetings to keep everyone and everything on track without causing a time drain and morale killing cycle of mindless meetings. At Microsoft and IBM, the two large companies where I once worked, there was a culture of meetings. A pretty substantial chunk of the work day was spent in meetings. There were several good and bad reasons for this and a range of positive and negative outcomes. First, the good: When people in a large complex matrix need to get something done, it requires coordination and clarity regarding responsibilities. This means meetings. You have to meet and assess who is doing what, what the schedule looks like, clarify misunderstandings, handle unexpected developments, and so on. When I was involved in doing public relations for a major acquisition at Microsoft, our group got together several times a week because a lot of very important, top secret stuff was flying around different departments at high speed.

On the downside, excessive meetings can take a major toll on the whole marketing effort – or really the entire organization. At Microsoft, the pattern is to set a sequence of weekly meetings for any project or team. In addition, managers typically hold a weekly one-on-one meeting with their direct reports. With this pattern, you can easily see your schedule fill up with twenty hours of meetings a week or more. This level of meeting frequency inevitably creates gridlock as regular work suffers. Some people actually sit in meetings doing other work on their laptops, or spend the entire time texting, while others stay late to finish their work after a day full of meetings. Overall, this is neither productive nor healthy, and contributes to bureaucracy and slow processes.

What is a possible solution? Meetings are essential but excessive meetings can get in the way of marketing effectiveness. I do not have an easy answer for a large matrixed organization, but one simple idea which will work well is to schedule <u>shorter</u> meetings. This sounds obvious, but it works. When I was involved in the acquisition deal at Microsoft, I needed to meet with the PR firm's team every day so I set a 10-minute catch-up call every day at 4PM. No need to drag everyone in for a half hour. However, in the same spirit, think carefully about occasionally booking your group for a full hour. Is it really necessary? I have been to several quadrillion meetings in my life. I think most meetings can be held in fifteen minutes if people are focused. The reflex to spend a half-hour or hour every time a team needs to meet is potentially wasteful.

Accountability

Accountability is one of the main goals of all of these plans, calendars, and meetings. Of course, the work itself is the primary objective. You have marketing to do and the plans and meetings exist to make sure it all gets done. The all-important subtext, however, is accountability. Who is responsible for this or that task? Does it get done on time and done properly? And, who deserves to be recognized and promoted for doing a good job, and who needs some constructive criticism about being more on task?

Task ownership is the basic unit of accountability. The detail sheet shown in Table 22 contains a column for ownership. The person who owns the task is accountable for getting it done, usually by an agreed-upon date. This is a very simple concept, though it is possible for things to become confusing when there are a lot of tasks, people and teams working in parallel. This is why you need the plan and calendar in sync with all these meetings. If you need to know what you are expected to do, look at the plan. If you need to know when to do it, look at the calendar. If you're not sure about it, the meeting is a great opportunity to talk it over.

If you're leading a team, you have a responsibility to the members to define and enforce accountability. Teams work better together if everyone understands their respective roles as well as the tasks and objectives for which they have accountability. I come to this knowledge because once even I was a pretty mediocre manager myself. This is a lesson I've had to learn and relearn the hard way a dozen times. How you implement accountability is a matter of personal style. I prefer having a dialogue about what people expect to be able to accomplish, then getting buy-in from them committing to ownership, based on their approval. Others are more dictatorial, which is not necessarily a bad thing. A lot of teams work well under an authoritarian leader with distinct boundaries and expectations. The working relationship is kept super clear.

The OARP

In a small company, responsibilities are (or should be) relatively easy to define. In a large, complex matrix, it can become a lot more complicated to figure out who is doing what and who is responsible for a given task.

Microsoft has a solution to this challenge. Though it is a bit cumbersome and bureaucratic, it deserves attention. It is called the OARP. OARP is an acronym for **O**wner, **A**pprover, **R**eviewer and **P**articipant. (I know, it sounds like Anger, Denial, Bargaining, Depression, and Acceptance the five stages of grief, but I digress.) The OARP brings together and clarifies the roles of the four main types of participants in any given project:

- Owner – The person(s) responsible and accountable for the work getting done.

- Approver – The person(s), typically the senior executive involved, who approves the work, which the participants and owners have done.

- Reviewer – Key stakeholders, often from matrixed groups, who are given the opportunity to review and comment on the work.

- Participant – The person(s) who actually do the work.

You might think this is overkill, and if you are not doing something significant like a big press release, it is probably excessive. But, OARP is a useful concept in managing a large group of people, some of whom are quite important but may have only a tangential involvement in the work being done. Consider what happens when a division of a company wants to issue a press release, which mentions another division. Under an OARP approach, the division which is mentioned in the release should get the right to be a reviewer or even an approver. Ignore such stakeholders at your peril! The OARP is also helpful because it clarifies what is expected of busy people. The average tech company executive's plate is way past full.

When you hear, in this case, that another division wants you involved in a press release they're putting out, your first reaction may justifiably be, "No! I can't handle anything else." However, if they are using OARP, they can tell you that they need your eyes on only two drafts of the document and nothing else. No meetings, no calls, etc. This process is a driver of efficiency in a large matrix.

Managing Up and Down

For a marketing manager at any level, getting work done involves skillful management in both up and down directions. In downward terms, you have to get your team organized and performing tasks on schedule and with accountability. Upwardly, you have to make sure the people to whom you are accountable understand what you are going to do and when you are going to do it. Managers do not like surprises. You do not want your team to surprise you with, "Hey, we're late. It was due yesterday and we could have warned you a week ago but the project won't be ready for another five days. It is not our fault..." Not good. "Firing-worthy" not good. Similarly, you do not want to be hanging your head as you reluctantly walk into a meeting with your boss, announcing that whatever you promised is late, incomplete, done wrong, etc.

Upward and downward management go together. The way you manage your team will affect how well you can manage your boss. If your team lacks accountability and you're not tracking their progress, you will be unable to know how to keep your boss informed about the status of the work you've promised to do. Regular communication is the key. Recurring team meetings keep you apprised of how things are going and give you the opportunity to get involved in decisions which affect the work. In my experience, there is an even more important result from recurring meetings and communication through the management layers. Repetition creates familiarity with what is going on, with the broad effect of getting everyone attuned to the work at hand. If you meet with your boss once and brief her on what you're doing, but then go silent for three months, there is no way she is going to remember what you're up to. A surprise or plan deviation will seem like a serious problem even if it isn't. If your boss has been updated regularly, your team's work will be part of her mental map of what is happening in the organization. Changes in plan and deliverables will flow naturally and be perceived as part of a well-understood bigger picture. You want to be in this positive position - not the former, where you come off as an unreliable creator of risk in the organization.

Channeling Francis Ford Coppola

Francis Coppola described the making of *Apocalypse Now* as coming from a process of bringing together "the script, the actors, and whatever happened to us in the jungle." So it is with technology marketing. We have our script, also known as our plan. We have the actors, which includes you, your team members, customers, and higher management. Next, we have the jungle. A lot of scary stuff can happen in the jungle. Most tech marketers make at least some of their work up as they go along. Usually, you don't have a choice. Any day you go to work the jungle could throw some serious challenges at you.

Responding to those challenges should bring out your inner Coppola. Will you make great art and win awards based on what happens in the jungle, or will you get devoured by tigers? The main thing to think about in the marketing jungle is what you should attack and what you should avoid. Marketers, like many other professionals in business, are constantly being flooded with potentially distracting tasks, which are forced on them. Some of these may be critical. Others are a waste of time. Marketers are particularly vulnerable given how subjective and creative the process can be. If you are a floor manager at a car factory, your boss probably won't come in one day and say "Hey, let's make SUVs today instead of sports cars."

However, in the flexible discipline of marketing, you will routinely be offered suggestions and potential mandates to change everything you're doing or tackle huge projects which may dynamite your whole plan.

You either take the assignment or pass. Passing may not be easy, but there will be times when you have to. If you took on every assignment in the jungle, you'd get swamped and accomplish nothing of substance. Your scorecard would be all red and your plan would be unrealized. At the same time, you have to remain open-minded and see the potential for transformation of your results through good ideas. This is where your plan and planning process is your secret weapon. If the suggested activity aligns with the plan and its strategy, you have the basis for agreeing with the idea, while pushing back and explaining that doing the new task will inevitably rob your existing plan of resources. Rejecting an idea can follow the same script. If the proposed new activity doesn't fit with the goals you've established with your managers, you have a good pretext for turning it down. Note: If you haven't vetted your plan with your manager, you will be easier to push around.

Tools

In the spirit of writing one paragraph to address a topic which has been the subject of numerous books, I wanted to comment about marketing management tools. Tools are optional, but realistically, you are going to need them to get your work done. Any marketing team which is connecting with other parties to accomplish tasks needs some digital organization. There are three basic types of software tools used for managing marketing:

- **Group collaboration tools** – Marketing almost always involves bringing groups of people together to perform tasks in concert. Inevitably, these people are not in the same location or even at the same company. Collaboration tools enable people to communicate and share files and tasks. Examples include Microsoft SharePoint, Jive Clearspace, and IBM Lotus Quickr.

- **Project management tools** – Marketers can take advantage of project management software, which enables groups to share project timelines, critical path task assignments, and more. Though these types of tools are designed for projects of any type – software development, construction, event planning – they have a lot of applicability in marketing. Microsoft Project is a great example of this type of tool.

- **Asset management tools** – Marketing generates a huge assortment of digital assets, such as images, logos, and video files. Software has evolved over the last decade or so to help marketers manage these assets. Sometimes called Digital Asset Management (DAM) or Marketing Asset Management (MAM) suites, they are basically databases connected to file storage directories. Most of these tools have version control and workflow capabilities, which enable a group of people to develop an asset, approve it, and store the correct version for future use. A lot of time is wasted by marketers looking for the right assets. DAM helps avoid this problem.

Many group collaboration tools combine all three functions. Microsoft SharePoint has group features, such as team sites, asset management, task assignment, calendaring, and so on. Standalone systems in each functional area tend to be more sophisticated, though the sophistication can be wasted on many marketing departments. This is not a knock on marketers. This is a reflection of reality. One of the great but gravely true clichés of software

196

use is, "the tool is only as good as its users." However, in marketing, there is a big Catch-22 which may get in the way of effective use of tools. Generally, the most successful scenarios for powerful, dedicated tools, such as enterprise DAM systems, involve teams committed to the tool for routine tasks over the long term. One example of this type of repetitive workflow is the creation of print advertisements. In this case, teams of people have to interact in flexible ways, but almost always following the same creation and approval processes.

Marketers almost never have this luxury. You're going to be using the tools with colleagues who work across the matrix or at other entities. They have likely never been trained in the use of some tools and won't want the aggravation. The tool will either be misused or circumvented. There is nothing funnier, and more tragic, than a group of people avoiding the ten million dollar system to send files to each other by email and wondering later why they can't find the right version.

My recommendation is to find the simplest, easiest tool for your marketing department. Ideally, this is free and familiar to most people. Or, it should be a tool so intuitive, users can teach themselves how to manage it in a few minutes. One of my most successful uses of a tool occurred during the crash preparation for a Bill Gates keynote address. Eight of us needed rapid access to a set of files and an evolving plan. The team was comprised of people from three internal divisions at Microsoft and two external agencies. We used Groove, now called SharePoint Workspaces. We had the team site up in about ten minutes. It was very much an instant learning experience, so within an hour we were all using the tool to share a plan and versions of the keynote speech. One challenge which Groove addressed in this case, was the need to cross organizational firewalls to achieve collaboration. This is a seemingly minor issue until you actually have to deal with it. If you have a project management solution which is not set up to handle users from more than one entity, you can be stuck. Newer, cloud-based tools make this a bit simpler to manage, though they can introduce security problems due to their openness.

CONCLUSION

My old mentor, the film and television producer Edgar Scherick, used to say, "Any fool can start a picture. It takes a wise man to end one." It is time to end this book; however I despise conclusions. Yet, they are necessary if you want to finish a piece of writing. Readers seem to want them and I hate to disappoint. The formula for a conclusion is well known: Recap what you have just said and then glance ahead to future developments and trends which may be relevant to the reader. Let's try it.

It is an Integrative, Iterative, Evolving Discipline

Here is my precise recap. B2B technology marketing is a fuzzy discipline. It integrates many different fields into one. You have lead generation, communications, branding and Internet marketing, all rolled up into one area of responsibility. And responsibility is the key word here. If you are doing B2B tech marketing, you are responsible for execution and accountable for the results you deliver. It is iterative. You keep going back to the same tasks over and over hoping to improve the outcomes with every new try. And, this is evolving - rapidly. Even some of the material in this book is already slipping into obsolescence in the two years it took me to write it.

An Industry in Flux

The fundamentals of B2B marketing never change. However, the specific practices and processes are shifting rapidly. The rise of social media and mobile apps, along with the impossible hype, are more significant factors in marketing than they were a year ago. Mobile marketing is growing more sophisticated and is starting to find a place in B2B technology marketing. Online advertising is becoming exponentially more advanced and will have an impact on B2B.

The corporate landscape has also shifted in the time it took to write this book. Apple was already in its ascendancy two years ago but the debut of the iPad has cemented the company's new status as one of the most valued corporations on earth. Apple's rise is affecting the entire industry. Partially as a result of Apple, but also because of other changes in the way technologies are created, devices in general are more important in the industry than they used to be. The paradigm of devices being relegated to commodity platforms for valuable software is under siege. Cloud computing is changing the way that companies buy IT services, hardware, and software. HP and Dell, two major players, which are struggling with these shifts, are searching for new, meaningful strategic directions. Microsoft also finds itself in catch-up mode. The day-to-day reality of the industry has changed.

It's All about You

Why should any of this matter? It matters, or at least it should matter, because ultimately this book is about you. I want you to be successful in your technology marketing endeavors. I hope that you read every part of this book with a mindset of "What is in it for me? Why should I care about this or that?" When we talk about communication, for example, think about how you are able to grow professionally and put yourself in a position to be promoted by being a great communicator. When we talk about generating sales leads or supporting sales, you might want to use the exercise to position yourself as a valued sales support person. Every aspect of B2B technology marketing can be viewed as an avenue of personal and professional growth.

I am bullish about the future of B2B technology marketing as a career. The field has changed, of course, and continues to evolve. The growth of increasingly complex matrices and third party partnerships makes figuring out how to have a successful career a bit challenging. However, if anything, the growth in complexity – as well as the inherent globalization involved – creates demand for more versatile and skilled marketers. Every tech company needs marketing people who know how to get the job done economically. They need you!

About the Author

Hugh Taylor has written marketing content for such clients as Microsoft, IBM, SAP, First Data, and Google. Hugh served as Social Software Evangelist at IBM Software Group, Public Relations Manager for Microsoft's SharePoint Technologies, and VP of Marketing and several early stage technology ventures. He is the author three books and dozens of articles and white papers about the interplay between business and technology. Hugh is also a frequent speaker at industry conferences. Prior to working in technology, Hugh was VP of Television Development at Edgar Scherick Associates. He earned his AB and MBA from Harvard. He lives in Los Angeles.

Made in the USA
Charleston, SC
17 January 2014